ABOUT THE AUTHOR

Miranda Holden is a psychotherapist, spiritual counsellor and interfaith minister. She is a leading light in the *A Course in Miracles* community and author of the *Soul Healing* meditation series. Miranda originally trained in her native Australia as a television presenter, but despite early media success re-trained to focus on her true passion of spirituality and inner transformation.

Throughout the early nineties Miranda held a thriving healing and counselling practice in England and, in 1996, she founded The Interfaith Seminary, a ground-breaking training for ministers and spiritual counsellors throughout Europe and America. A gifted speaker, Miranda gives public workshops and inspirational talks internationally on themes of spirituality, transformation and relationships. She is married to Robert Holden, author and creator of The Happiness Project, and lives in Oxford, England.

BOUNDLESS LOVE

Transforming your life
with grace and inspiration

Miranda Holden

RIDER

LONDON · SYDNEY · AUCKLAND · JOHANNESBURG

5 7 9 10 8 6

Published in 2002 by Rider,
an imprint of Ebury Press, Random House,
20 Vauxhall Bridge Road, London SW1V 2SA
www.randomhouse.co.uk

Random House Australia (Pty) Limited
20 Alfred Street, Milsons Point, Sydney,
New South Wales 2061, Australia

Random House New Zealand Limited
18 Poland Road, Glenfield,
Auckland 10, New Zealand

Random House South Africa (Pty) Limited
Isle of Houghton, Corner of Boundary Road & Carse O'Gowrie,
Houghton 2198, South Africa

The Random House Group Limited Reg. No. 954009

Papers used by Rider are natural, recyclable products
made from wood grown in sustainable forests.

Printed and bound in England by
Antony Rowe Ltd Chippenham, Wiltshire

A CIP catalogue record for this book
is available from the British Library

ISBN 9780712614344 (from Jan 2007)
ISBN 0-7126-1434-6

Contents

Acknowledgements

Gratitude To:

The Spirit of Boundless Love, which has moved me, healed me and carried me all through my life.

My wise and wonderful husband Robert, my soul-mate whose love is reflected on every page.

My family, whom I treasure as unique and precious jewels, for their love.

My English family Sally and David Holden, whose love and support has always been unhesitating.

Students, graduates, mentors, facilitators and trustees of The Interfaith Seminary, whose presence feeds me with inspiration, healing and soul companionship along the way.

My brilliant and gifted Interfaith Seminary colleagues Peter Dewey, Elaine Walker, Mike Steward and Fay Barratt, for their wisdom, humility, and for lightening my load so I could write.

The New Seminary USA community, and especially Diane Berke, for her inspiration, friendship and generosity of spirit.

My editor Judith Kendra, for her kind encouragement and faith in me.

My assistant Sharon Willis, for her efficient, practical support, and my previous assistant Kimberly Chepey, for her soul sisterhood.

Susan Jeffers, Alan Cohen and Paul Wilson, for their friendship, inspiration and kind endorsement of my work.

Tom and Linda Carpenter, for their exceptional living example of Boundless Love, which constantly inspires me to be ever-clearer in my intention, and ever-more committed to the ways of love.

The many teachers and authors I have been blessed to learn from, who have encouraged me to be spiritually bold over the years.

My friends, especially Anna Pasternak and Deirdre O'Flynn, for invaluable, honest feedback. Kathy and Bob Coleman, for being such great playmates. Ben and Veronica Renshaw and Avril Carson and Charlie Shand, for their support and unquestioning friendship. Jennifer and Neil Hopley, for their kinship. Lisa Corser and family, for their love and hospitality. Justine Silver, for her laughter and loving care. Ian Patrick, for his support and willingness. Julie Wookey, for being such a sister in love. Sue and Jeff Allen, for their strength and tenderness. Chuck Spezzano, for his great compassion, and Lency Spezzano, whose love midwifed me through a particularly dark night.

Everyone who has attended private spiritual counselling sessions and public workshops over the years, for opening my eyes to see the Divine more clearly.

Everyone in the world who is courageously choosing to open their heart to the Boundless, hold faith in the goodness of humanity and reach out to others with love.

To Coleman Barks, for kind permission to quote his poetry translations from *Lalla: Naked Song*, published by Maypop Books 1992. To Daniel Ladinsky, for his permission to quote Hafiz poems from three volumes: *The Gift: Poems by Hafiz*, published by Penguin 1999; *The Subject Tonight is Love: 60 Wild and Sweet Poems of Hafiz*, published by Penguin 1996, and *I Heard God Laughing: Renderings of Hafiz*, published by Sufism Reoriented 1996, Walnut Creek, CA 94595.

* All case histories that appear in this book are actual not fictional, though some names have been altered to protect confidentiality where requested.

Part I

YOUR
AWAKENING

Boundless vision

'You have been invited to meet "The Friend".
No one can resist a Divine Invitation
That narrows all our choices to just two:
We can come to God dressed for dancing,
Or be carried on a stretcher to God's ward.'

Hafiz – 14th-century Sufi poet

Wherever you are on life's road, no matter what's happened to you, how young or old you are, whether you regard yourself as on a spiritual path or not, Boundless Love has something huge to offer you. Boundless Love is the experience of God and your true Self. It brings you home to your inherent wholeness. It is never too late to re-gain it, and your past is irrelevant. It offers you a practical spiritual map to profound joy and peace, beyond the boundaries of your fears, pains and limitations. To the soul, life is all about waking up into the reality of Boundless Love.

I was raised in suburban Perth, Australia. Spirituality played no real part in my family life. That said, as a small child I lived in an interior world of enchantment and interconnectedness with all things. Realms beyond the physical senses were natural to me. Unusually sensitive, I could feel what other people were feeling and seemed to know their innermost thoughts. Yet even then I felt a longing to return to something I seemed to be gradually losing. I hovered between bliss and deep loneliness. Playing on the beach and enjoying the great outdoors, I looked outwardly like any other kid my age, but inwardly I was always pondering the deeper meaning of things.

At the age of seven I pestered my parents to let me go to church with the family next door. I remember being so excited, thinking that perhaps this would re-connect me with the inner vision that had made life so joyous when I was really small. Sitting in the pews waiting for the service to begin I closed my eyes for a moment. I felt a wave of luminous love blow through me. Somehow, I knew it as the presence of God. It was so beautiful, natural and completely familiar, but the service that followed left me very confused. It felt dead, fearful and heavy – the complete opposite of the heaven I had just tasted. Although I loved the Biblical stories, I couldn't connect with the dogma, and decided then that conventional religion was not the way for me.

Meanwhile, home life was brewing up an increasingly explosive cauldron of anger, grievances, resentment, sacrifice and fear. It was impossible to be unaffected while living in an emotional war zone. My parents were good people in a bad relationship, and under tremendous financial pressure. Although they were extremely honourable and committed to my brother, sister and me, the dynamics taking place left me feeling powerless and isolated.

As I approached adolescence, it seemed that everywhere I turned was a desert of struggle and pain. The light I once knew was rapidly fading. I remember grieving for a love I now seemed so removed from. I yearned for someone or something to reach into my heart and tell me that this was all just a bad dream; that hope hadn't disappeared. These feelings were intense yet I lacked the emotional literacy to communicate and ask for help. Like many teenagers, I felt so profoundly alone and separate I doubted anyone could begin to understand my angst. Inside I was screaming, yet externally I couldn't make a sound. I was nick-named 'Miranda Mouse'. I was the one in the family who didn't cause trouble.

My difficulties were compounded by a move from my cosy, nurturing junior school to a prestigious, expensive, single sex senior school. To my horror, I had landed in 'bitch city'. In this pubescent soup of competition, comparison and jealousy, I felt more alone than I would have thought possible. By the time I was 13 years old I had lost faith in life and saw no other option but to withdraw and shut down: anything to get out of this hell. Silently, I snapped.

It took a while for the doctors to work out that my problems were emotional not physical. I was admitted to an adult psychiatric unit – despite my withdrawal I was considered 13 going on 35. I spent the next three months there. In this temple of suffering I was just one of many people unable to cope with the world I looked out upon. I shared a room with several women who had made attempts on their life, and witnessed the kinds of human suffering few 13-year-olds see, indeed few adults see. I was up close to narcotic withdrawal, schizophrenic and psychotic episodes, bleak and manic depression, and all other kinds of heart-break. In retrospect, I see that it was the perfect place for me to have been. I learnt about the deepest needs of the human heart, and most of all I learnt compassion.

Learning to surrender

I spent most of my days lying in bed staring out of the window. The energy and ethos of the staff was focused on containing the despair rather than providing a forum for healing its causes. They kept a distinct emotional and psychic distance from the patients. It was very much a case of 'us' and 'them'. Consequently we were heavily medicated and left to our own devices. All I wanted to do was to die. At my darkest moment, I remember praying to God – whom I didn't even know whether I believed in – 'Please let me die, please God let me die, get me out of here.'

That same afternoon, towards the end of my stay in the psychiatric unit, a miracle occurred. In my exhaustion, I just let go of everything, even wanting to die. In this moment of profound surrender, it was as though the room exploded with light and a thousand angels came to breathe life back into me. This experience viscerally reinstalled the glimpses of eternity I had as a young child. I felt like I had been lifted above the battleground of life into a whole new zone. There I was graced with an explicit vision of what is unalterably real. This insight enabled me to see with complete clarity.

Love is real

Much more than simply an emotion, love is the ultimate universal truth. Underneath all pain, problems and suffering, love shines unchanged at the core of all things. Though we may remove ourselves from love, love never departs.

God exists as Boundless Love

Not a righteous father figure in the sky, but an energy field of unconditional acceptance, a presence that pervades all things. All life lives and moves within God. Ultimately, all returns to God.

Our essence is Boundless Love

Like rays of light extending out from the sun, our essence is an extension of God's Boundless Love. No matter what trauma we go through in life, whether we forget or overlook our spiritual nature – the love we truly are – our wholeness remains. Therefore our capacity for peace and joy is forever intact.

Our ultimate purpose in life is to be the presence of Boundless Love

At the highest level, life is a process of spiritual evolution. We are not here solely to further our careers, accrue possessions, pay off the mortgage or even propagate the species. We are here to dissolve our barriers to love.

Allow everything to open you

Awakening to the love that we are and the love we have come to offer brings us true happiness. Opening to the spiritual vision of Boundless Love, healing whatever gets in the way of love, stretching our hearts to receive more love, anchoring our minds in the ways of love, and evolving our capacity to give only love is the directive that makes life truly work.

With this vision, I knew that I could handle whatever happened to me. I tasted heaven behind our earthly struggles and saw the light that never ceases. I do not exaggerate when I say that what I experienced was perfect order, perfect bliss.

Whether I stayed in this state for seconds, minutes or hours I do not know. Time ceased to have relevance. Like a light plug being put into the socket and the switch turned on, I had been spiritually reconnected. This experience gave me exactly what I needed to commit to life, to engage again, and to let my family's love reach me, if not completely, then a little bit more. With this vision, life was hopeful and potentially thrilling.

Today I look back on my breakdown and the subsequent cracking open of my heart, mind and soul as the most perfectly orchestrated catalyst for a life of spiritual service. I would not have had the motivation to dig broad and deep for the wisdom that has shaped me had I not experienced such hell. It accelerated my personal and spiritual growth and I am tremendously grateful for every part of it.

I invite you to consider that the greatest difficulty you have had to face is actually a perfect set-up for you to discover your true purpose in life. Often a spiritual breakthrough comes through some kind of shock or trauma when we are most broken, most on our knees. That is the moment to find the willingness to give up fighting and trying to control. When you have exhausted all other resources and have no energy – surrender. God's grace will catch you.

The more we let go, the easier it is to retrieve the gifts that always lie in direct proportion to any suffering. Luminous pearls grow out of a piece of grit in an oyster shell. Crises can be powerful opportunities for positive change, but extreme openings are not mandatory for a spiritual breakthrough. Everyone's awakening is unique. Don't judge the form yours takes. Whatever you may be facing now, don't assume it is a disaster. Perhaps it is trying to open you to something extraordinarily wonderful.

Your consciousness determines everything

After this visionary opening, my 'recovery' was pretty much instantaneous, and I was soon discharged from hospital. I returned to the same environment that had been so painful before, and although I did not have the power to change my situation, the grace I felt within allowed me to cope with it. I knew that beyond the various dramas everyone was going through there was another reality. I knew for certain that life did not need to be a struggle. I learnt that my consciousness, not my circumstances, determined my experience. I was determined to find the way to turn the vision of Boundless Love into my everyday experience. Hence, at 13 years of age, my spiritual journey actively began.

Throughout my teens I read any spiritual books I could get my hands on, from astrology, healing and esoteric material to Eastern philosophy and various great scriptures. I found a wonderful yoga teacher and began going to classes most days. By my late teens I was at meditation groups and personal growth seminars most evenings and weekends. I explored Buddhist meditation and philosophy, Sufi practice, metaphysics, theosophy, re-birthing, tarot, New Thought and every major personal development seminar going. If it was available, I tried it: the weird and the genuinely wise. Although I fell into many common traps it was a time of rapid assimilation, growth and learning.

My first few years exploring spiritual principles and practices were very exciting. A new doorway was opening and with it new hope and endless possibilities, but I began to recognise that I had to find a way of harnessing the vision of Boundless Love to begin changing the painful situations I repeatedly found myself in. Lofty visions were useless if I continued falling into the same ditches when I hit the ground. My ditches were all related to my shattered sense of Self, connected to unresolved wounds around my family, and beginning to play themselves out in painful relationships with men. A shift in emphasis was needed.

Seeking a deeper transformation

I realised that a spiritual perspective had the potential to become either a subtle means of escaping from our difficulties or a means to transform them. A friend I respected asked, *'Do you really seek the truth or are you wanting a spiritual anaesthetic?'* On closer inspection I saw too many people who had been on their spiritual path much longer than I whose lives were still a mess, even a little narcissistic; people who were estranged from their families and still trapped in limiting emotional patterns from their unresolved past. Their lives were just glossed with loving words and appearances of spirituality. In actuality, nothing really had changed.

I met only a few who had the courage to take what they discovered in their exploration to the most wounded parts of themselves and consistently apply the principles and practices where it matters most. They were the ones who really inspired me. They radiated something different: something pure and true.

They had loving relationships and families, their lives worked and they were creative, authentic, giving, abundant *and happy*. I met both kinds of people in every spiritual tradition I studied. I saw the same results of various material approached through superficial understanding or more courageous, honest application. My choice was clear. The light of my spirit had been switched on, only to reveal that the rooms of my life needed cleaning up. I got to work.

Once I committed to spiritual practice as a means for deep transformation, my life circumstances began to change for the better. The following quote from the psycho/spiritual text *A Course in Miracles* was my guiding light:

> 'Seek not for love; rather, seek to remove the blocks to the awareness of love's presence.'

My daily meditations and prayers were now tuned towards the unravelling of my wounds and false beliefs. I became less interested in the showier aspects of spirituality and more interested in how to apply the universal spiritual principles of unconditional acceptance, forgiveness, compassion, love and kindness to myself and others. This was a real stretch, especially when facing deep hurt, anger, betrayal, rejection or attack, but the results began to speak for themselves through increased personal power, serenity and, above all, a greater capacity to love.

The tangible shift in my awareness motivated me to commit more deeply to my spirituality. This began to threaten the relationship I was in at the time, which I eventually realised had no room in it for me to be spiritually authentic. After a messy break-up I spent three days reflecting and meditating on my true way forward – how to integrate my spiritual vision into relationships and everyday life. I realised that for me, living my spirituality was my central priority. I made a promise to myself that nothing would deter me from my calling and trusted it would lead me to a truer way of being in relationships.

Within that week, I met Robert. Falling deeply in love is inherently glorious, but in addition I was joining forces with someone who was as passionately committed to the truth of love as I. Our relationship amplified both of our awareness enormously. Two minds joined with the same intention can move mountains. We married nine months later. We began to meditate and pray together daily, sharing our discoveries and mirroring one another's blind spots, loving the wounds out of one another and giving one another courage to keep committing to the Boundless, even when we were resistant. It was intensely healing and utterly fabulous.

The Interfaith Seminary

Along the stages of my journey, more and more people would naturally gravitate to me for help, so I began to train in various forms of healing and psycho-therapeutic modalities. My own need for healing the obstacles to Boundless Love unintentionally became my full time work. Serving others seemed the most natural way to integrate and deepen what I was learning. From my early twenties I worked in private practice as a healer, spiritual counsellor and inspirational speaker, supporting others in diving within their own heart for wisdom. A desire for further study led me to enrol in an interfaith training called The Interfaith Seminary in New York, and to my own amazement I was ordained in 1995.

The following year I founded The Interfaith Seminary, dedicated to training Interfaith Ministers and Spiritual Counsellors. People who regard themselves as spiritual but not exclusively affiliated with one particular religion, those with a universal spiritual vision and those who find themselves on the fringes of their religion need someone they can trust to guide them through major life change, crisis, birth, marriage and death. I set up this programme to train open-hearted, inclusive spiritual guides. The programme struck a mighty chord and took off beyond what I could have anticipated, drawing people from all over Europe from all age ranges, professional backgrounds and walks of life.

For two years participants undergo an intensely experiential journey into universal truth, exploring world religions, mystical traditions, service, healing principles and how to apply them. Seeking oneness, the golden thread that underpins all genuine teachings, while also embracing the enrichment that differences can bring, they review and deepen their relationship to the

Boundless, to themselves and others. Encouraged to explore rather than to swallow dogma, they focus on rooting out their own judgements and intolerances, which create barriers to loving and accepting all. The level of spiritual awakening, healing and wisdom that arises is profound.

My passion is to guide people back into the Boundless Love within them. I believe that the human heart is God's birthing chamber. A friend once said to me that to see another truly is to be, 'On your knees in awe at the immense beauty before you.' Through directing The Interfaith Seminary, and facilitating countless retreats, public seminars and private sessions internationally, I have been privileged to midwife extraordinary levels of transformation in individuals, and subsequently their families and communities through spiritual practices and principles. In this book I share with you some of the most powerful methods that I know for personal awakening and transformation, and ultimately planetary healing, all kindly road tested by the Interfaith Seminary students, workshop participants, friends and clients over the years.

The truth of Boundless Love

Spiritual practice in one form or another has been the driving force in my life for the last 20 years. As I reflect upon my early awakening, I see that the vision I was opened to in my darkest hour in that psychiatric unit has been my guiding light throughout. It sustained me in difficult times and, as I learned to work with it, transformed and informed every area of my life. It constantly reminds me to remember the truth of Boundless Love. I have come to see there is nothing else. My hope is that this book connects you more directly to your own spiritual vision in a way that is powerful, authentic and useful.

In my heart of hearts I am a feminine mystic. I have not tried to edit that from this book. However, I am also a practically minded 'Aussie Sheila' who is ultimately interested in what really works to transform people's lives for the better. The Native American elder Sun Bear used to say, 'Do not bother me with your visions unless they grow corn.' My aim is to de-mystify the mystical and give you real tools.

The biggest joke of all is the Western world-view that spirituality is a luxury, not a necessity. A true spiritual life is immeasurably practical. No method of psychology I have explored has come close to being as powerful as spiritual principles in healing problems, and replacing those problems with purpose, passion, joy and meaning. Grace – the experience of God's Boundless Love – can heal what the human mind cannot.

Only spiritual maps can take you beyond the conscious, subconscious and unconscious mind into what some call the superconscious mind. This is the zone within you where miracles are natural and abundant. Drawing forward its limitless resources into your everyday experience is the most effortless way I know to effect real change in your life. Spiritual practices are your miracle-kit to gain access to grace. In the forthcoming chapters, I lead you through some of the most effective principles and practices I know. Embrace them, and they will help you to experience, be and offer Boundless Love.

You don't have to have an existing practice or faith, although if you do this book will help you build upon it. You are asked only to surrender. Surrender is an act of great courage, not weakness. It is not something you do only when you have no choice. Surrender daily, beginning from now. Surrender your fears, your expectations, your past, your sense of Self, your future, and make way for a beautiful vision, an eternal vision. Be willing to let God's Boundless Love find you. Have no doubt that somehow, it will.

What do you yearn for?

'No genuine longing can remain unfulfilled.'

Kahil Gibran

Recent scientific studies have shown that people with a strong spiritual vision live longer, happier, healthier lives. Mystics through the ages have demonstrated that beyond ordinary sense awareness lie limitless Divine resources for wisdom, strength, compassion, joy and peace. Listening to your soul's deepest yearnings will lead you directly into your boundless vision, giving new depth and direction to your whole life.

Something prompted my friend Jane to ask me to create a blessing ceremony for her children. I was delighted but surprised. Jane is a loving, practical-minded, down-to-earth person who clearly had a natural wisdom but had never wanted to talk about spiritual matters before. I gave Jane and her husband a series of questions to help name their vision of how they wanted to raise their family, so that I could create a tailor-made ceremony to support them. Some of these questions included:

* What has the birth of your children opened up in you?
* What are your greatest hopes and fears of parenthood?
* What, from your own upbringings, do you want to emulate for your children?
* What, from your own upbringings, do you want to forgive and do differently?
* What spiritual values would you like your children to grow up with?

Jane found these questions about the specific subtleties she wanted to pass onto her children difficult, a little threatening even. It demanded she explore the yearnings of her soul. Talking it through she told me that the whole arena of spirituality felt beyond her. It was something she knew nothing of, didn't have language for, didn't understand and had therefore negated. The cynical part of Jane regarded spiritual pursuits as an escape from the daily struggles of earning a living and raising a family. Underneath her cynicism, Jane wondered whether there was a void where her soul should be.

It was clear to me that the Boundless was no stranger to Jane. It's just that her experiences were moments within the ordinary rather than blinding flashes of light. This led to a powerful conversation about Jane's spirituality. Distinct from the beliefs and creeds of religion, spirituality is about direct personal contact with the Boundless. Sometimes this can occur within a religious structure, but often it doesn't. Each person will experience it uniquely. There is no right or wrong way to experience God.

Jane could identify the unconditional love she felt for her children and husband as sacred. Additionally, Jane spoke of a presence which she sensed had sheltered her from harm's way in potentially dangerous situations, moments of reaching out to ease another's suffering as a nurse and feeling a wave of something beyond herself, and of moments of wonder within nature. Taking the time to explore her soul yearnings and recognise her moments of grace allowed Jane to access her unique spirituality. God is substantial, but subtle. Don't make the mistake of thinking that if your sense of spirituality does not fit into a particular box, it is not there. There is no time, place or state where God is absent.

What is your experience of God?

This question is the opening conversation we have on the very first day of the Interfaith Seminary training. It always opens profound doorways. If you search your life thoroughly, there will have been moments when you seemed to touch upon something beyond your ordinary sense awareness. Moments in which you knew you were more than just your body, your personality, your nationality, your family or cultural heritage, your sex, even your mind.

Perhaps you felt it alone in nature, in the birth of your child, at a dying loved one's bedside, in a magical moment with someone precious to you, in an unexpected synchronicity, or a time when somehow your heart broke out of its usual cage. Boundless moments where you felt graced with a sense of awe, humility, gratitude, wonder and joy, even if just for a split second. Nurture rather than negate your glimpses of God. They are your keys to a deeper, sweeter life.

Unless we know what for us, personally, is most sacred, life will lack focus, and we will stay within the lower reaches of our mind where fear, guilt and lack rule. Life will lack luminosity and subtle texture, blocking us from fulfilling our true potential. A lack of spiritual clarity can cause us to feel that nothing we do, nothing we are given and no one we are with is quite 'enough'. Our capacity to receive is inhibited, which takes us out of the natural flow and makes life feel harder than it needs to be. This can leave us with the vague feeling that we are living life in third gear.

Exploring more deeply your own sacred vision opens the doorway to a whole new way of being. Vast capacities for love, joy, freedom and brilliance reside untapped within your soul. Connecting with your deepest yearnings clarifies your spirituality and initiates a truer, freer existence, evoking the Boundless Love within you to bless and serve others. In listening to the longings of countless people over the years, the following themes seem to be perennial. I suggest you sit with them quietly, making note of your responses on paper. See which elements recur for you. Let them lead you to a greater definition of what it is you seek.

The longing for connection

Everyone yearns to belong to something beyond their individual Self. We look to belong, be bonded to and be understood as young children within our family, as a teenager with our peer group, then in adulthood with a lover or life-partner, and professionally with friends, colleagues and our work community. This mirrors the soul's yearning to feel connected with the source of all that is. Driving this is a deep longing to return to a state of awareness beyond separation. The ancient echo of oneness reverberates from deep within, although we seem to wander the world in the illusion that we are separate.

At the centre of all mystic traditions is this longing for re-connection. Christian mystics spoke of it as the sacred marriage between Self and Creator, Sufis as the communion between Lover and Beloved. To Jewish mystics the two triangles of the star of David depicts the longing for unity between the Boundless and humanity. Separation is the primary illusion that all spiritual paths aim to awaken us from.

Ask yourself:
* What helps me feel connected? Less alone?
* What helps me feel at one with my Self? With The Infinite? With others?

The longing for unconditional love

It is universally acknowledged that infants need love and affection in order to develop optimally. At what age are human beings supposed to grow out of this need? Whatever age or stage you are in life, you need love like you need oxygen. Love is an awareness that sustains your soul, and is not dependent on external circumstances. Love is your heritage and the heart of who you are. Love knows no judgement, condemnation or conditions. Unconditional love is one and the same as total acceptance. It is an experience of being championed and believed in, no matter what may unfold.

Whatever has occurred in the story line of your life, you know love. It came with you into this world. Your memory of it may have waned, but underneath your disappointments and heart-breaks the light of Boundless Love glimmers. Kindle your memory of being held within the embrace of Love itself and you will gradually become aware that you rest there still, and will do so forever.

Ask yourself:
* What is my source of unconditional love?
* What helps me to feel unconditional love?
* What helps me to give unconditional love?

The longing for deep peace

The saying, 'Stop the world, I want to get off', speaks directly to the craving for a deep inner rest: a desire for struggle, battle, competition, fear and stress to end. Drawing life's external dramas to a halt requires you to stop the war within. No matter how stressful your life is at present, peace is within you now. It shines like a tiny star in the heavens of your mind. You need not seek for peace, simply stop resisting and fighting the way things are, that you may access it.

Ask yourself:
* *What truly gives me peace?*
* *What am I insisting I need to get done before I can be at peace?*
* *What helps me to be still?*

The longing for pure joy

Something deep within us suspects we were built for Boundless Bliss. Our desire for fun, laughter, outrageousness, pleasure, even sex is a mirror of our soul's longing for spiritual ecstasy and rapture. Our soul craves to abandon the sense of reserve, throw caution to the wind and play big. The Hindu saints Sri Anandamayi Ma and Ramakrishna, and the Sufi mystics Hafiz and Rumi embodied the rapturous aspect of spirituality, existing in states of pure joy 'drunk on light'. The precursor to joyous, rapturous states of being is gratitude. The kind that makes your heart feel physiologically bigger.

Ask yourself:
* *What makes my heart sing with joy?*
* *What makes me come alive?*
* *What am I truly grateful for?*

The longing for inner freedom

Life in the physical realm can sometimes feel very restricting to the soul. Within us is the knowledge that we are more than our bodies. Life on earth can feel very dense at times. The longing for a sense of freedom and limitlessness beyond duality and physical boundaries comes from a soul memory of total boundlessness. The Yogis called this Mukti – the soul yearning to be free from fears, inner limitations, blocks, doubts, old wounds, rules and inner barriers that restrict the real you.

Ask yourself:
* *What exactly do I yearn to be free from?*
* *What makes me feel limitless?*
* *What helps me remember that I am free?*

The longing to come home

I have yet to meet a person who has never had moments when they felt a stranger in this world. A passage from *A Course in Miracles* says, 'This world you seem to live in is not home to you. And somewhere in your mind you know that this is true. A memory of home keeps haunting you, as if there were a place that called you to return, although you do not recognise the voice, nor what it is the voice reminds you of.' Often we confuse spiritual homesickness with the need to be in a different physical place, when really the soul simply seeks a more unified state of being.

Ask yourself:
* *What gives me a sense of being at home?*
* *What is home to me?*

The longing for timelessness

At the Interfaith Seminary we explore myriad ways of communing with the Divine. A practice that moves everyone deeply is a Sufi chant and dance to the words 'Ya Quayum'. This translates from Arabic as, 'towards the eternal'. The second part to it are the words, 'Timeless, timeless, I am free.' Such is the soul's longing to rest in its natural state in the eternal present, not in past and future references, that this chant sends the group into levels of deep resonance. Our soul is ageless and timeless. Even when our bodies die our essence will live forever. Reality is changeless.

Ask yourself:
* *What supports me in being completely present?*
* *What doesn't change?*
* *What has the breath of the eternal upon it?*

Embrace your soul longings

Do not dismiss your soul longings as irrelevant or impractical. They are your spiritual blueprints, your keys into a more immediate experience of Boundless Love. Nurture them and pay attention to where they want to draw you.

Your longings highlight your truest needs. Do not despair that they are beyond your reach. Just do not look to the world to fulfil them for you. Every great sage, from Jesus to Buddha, guided humanity to focus on recovering our true identity and its inner riches. Possessions, worldly achievements and outer circumstances are to your soul what a non-fat meal is to your body – they just doesn't leave you feeling satisfied. Enjoy what the world can give, play with it, but know its gifts are temporary and limited. Listening to your soul longings will lead you to a truer fulfilment, leading you to connect more deeply with a truer source of sustenance. This gives you boundless new resources with which to change your life and transform difficulties.

Do not fear looking within

The fulfilment and answers you seek are within you, but are you looking there? Are you afraid of the Pandora's box it may open? Do you have a hidden fear that yielding to the Boundless would mean some kind of destruction, loss of self and all that you have created your life to be? If so, you would not be unusual. It is human nature to try to stay with what we know, even when it is painful or dissatisfying.

Like sitting before a sumptuous banquet but not eating of it, resistance to going within can leave us longing for union, yet running from it, seeking but never finding. We can easily get caught up in worldly values of trying to prove ourselves and accumulate more to fill what is essentially a hunger for spiritual love. Looking to the outside world for substitutes to keep our fears of what we may find within hidden, we can find ourselves being led further away from our soul's true axis.

Our substitutes for the experience of Boundless Love can take many forms, at best echoing our yearning for union with the source, at worst numbing the yearning out of our mind. The search to find a 'soul mate', a special relationship where we can feel united in loving and being loved by another, is a mirror of our longing to experience Divine union once again. So, too, is our drive to achieve wealth, security, fame or that which we think will make our world safe. None of these goals are inherently bad, although if our fundamental intention is to make our partners, children, career or ambition the source of our fulfilment, then we will inevitably wind up dissatisfied and looking for the next carrot to chase. I have counselled countless people who in the world's eyes 'have it all', yet no matter how much fame, love, success, money and adoration they accrue, they feel lacking without an inner spiritual compass.

Be still and know

Have you ever tried to come off caffeine, sugar, alcohol, junk food or cigarettes? For the first week, when your body is elimi- nating the toxins, you can feel awful, but before long you begin to feel calmer, clearer and more vibrant. Similarly, sages from every tradition have guided seekers into deeper spiritual waters by first encouraging them to slow down. This means literally doing less and reflecting more.

Boundless Love is always present, but you are not always attuned to receive it. Whatever level you find yourself spiritual- ly, by creating more space in your life, sitting quietly more often, even reminding yourself to take deep breaths throughout your activities, you will find yourself coming into greater harmony with the subtleties of life, becoming less reactive to events around you. This naturally precludes a greater sense of stillness, supporting your capacity to absorb a new way of being. Know that whatever you leave empty, God will fill. You can find what you have really been looking for. The following meditation is designed to give you a taste of the Boundless Love that is available. Go over it now, and again just before you go to bed tonight.

Opening the door of your longings: a meditation

Sit somewhere quiet and comfortable where you will not be disturbed. Close your eyes. Turn your attention within. Breathe and consciously allow your body to relax more and more with each exhale. As you soften inwards, feel into the longings you have identified.

⤏ Feel something within drawing you to turn around within your mind. As you do so, you see a staircase leading up to a doorway. Beams of light peep through the cracks of this doorway. These beams of light call to your deepest yearnings, and you are drawn to walk up the staircase to that doorway.

⤏ Behind this door is a taste of everything you truly want, the source that can truly fulfil your deepest needs. Place your hand on the knob, open the door and walk over the threshold into the light on the other side of the doorway . . . . Just let yourself absorb whatever the Boundless offers you here. Be open and receive. What do you see? What do you feel? What sounds do you hear? Who is there with you?

⤏ In your own time, return to the awareness of where you are sitting, through taking a few deeper breaths and gently opening your eyes. Know that the doorway to the fulfilment of your soul's deepest longings has been kept deliberately open.

'Look within, thou art the Buddha.' *Zen proverb*

'The kingdom of heaven is within you.' *Jesus*

'In the depths of the soul, one sees the Divine.' *Tao te Ching*

Spiritual de-toxing

Any thought of God that is not loving is a lie.

For years I avoided the word 'God'. It conjured up negative images taught to me by a fearful religious education teacher at school. Her God was very conditional – loving if you behaved yourself; wrathful if you had too much fun. This zealous teacher spread a gospel of guilt about pop music, sexuality, late night television, eating too many biscuits, and just about everything enjoyable. She tried to impress upon us that anything other than her religion was 'Satan worship', which would land us in the fires of hell. It was heavy stuff for a nine-year-old. I was terrified and turned off.

Hence the word 'God' just wasn't hip! I side-stepped the issue, preferring other terms that were not so charged, like 'The Universe', 'Great Spirit' or 'the Source'. That way I could distance myself from religious connotations and theology, which I had rejected as false. The Eastern traditions of yoga, Buddhism and the Tao were a lot more comfortable. 'The Universe', however, felt a bit vague, abstract and hard to get a handle on. Sometimes you need a better grip. I realised that if I wanted to feel Boundless Love more intimately I had to de-tox my religious conditioning. Doing so bonded me with a vast power that I could rely upon for support and guidance whenever I reached the end of myself.

Calling God by a different name before you have released past negative associations with the word 'God' is the spiritual equivalent of brushing pink paint onto a cracked wall. Freeing yourself from past toxic or fearful indoctrination creates a stronger foundation that rebirths your spirituality into a new level of authenticity and inspiration. Furthermore, it brings you the capacity to discern the universal pearls from superstitious religious dogma. Healing your religious past ensures that your spirituality becomes a genuine force for transformation, not a subtle act of rebellion.

No single religion, culture or group has a monopoly on the Boundless. Truth is one, paths are many. Call it what you like: Love, God, Goddess, Spirit, Adonai, Allah, Christ, Source, Buddha nature, Brahma, The Tao, The Universe, Mother or Father, God doesn't care. Beyond convictions or conventions, no language can truly describe a living experience that is wordless. God is not a person with an ego and does not take offence. Yet, since the beginning of time, humanity's different spiritual perceptions and understandings have caused division and needless suffering. Tragically, they still do.

Fundamentally, we seek the same experience. The problem is never in our different understandings of God, but forgetting to live the principles of our path in our interaction with others. Any true spiritual practice will cleanse the heart of hatred, guilt and fear, producing greater capacities for kindness, wisdom and love.

A Buddhist, Hindu, Christian, Muslim, Jew, Taoist, Sikh, Metaphysician, Shaman or even atheist need have no difficulty in experiencing real kinship with one another if they are truly practising the essence of their teaching instead of defending it. All that really matters is whether or not your spirituality supports you in living the truth of your being, whether it makes you a curse or blessing to the world.

Commit to a spirituality that supports you

Begin your spiritual de-toxification now. Find a notebook to use as a journal, and write in your own words the relationship you would like to have with the Boundless.

Name your intention. For example:

* 'I commit to a deeper experience of God and my true self.'
* 'I want to know that I am unconditionally loved and supported by God.'
* 'I want to find my true spiritual path.'

Having named your goal, commit to it. Let it become your true north. Ask to be guided towards its actuality.

I have yet to meet a true atheist, only people disillusioned with religion. It is easy to feel disconnected from a sense of higher meaning, upset at feeling abandoned by God in a sometimes harsh world, confused by contradictory scripture, turned off by horrendous acts perpetrated in the name of God, repulsed by clerical abuse of power. Understandable though this is, none of it has anything to do with the real God and everything to do with our projections onto God. God has been given an extremely bad PR.

At the Interfaith Seminary, we run a session early on in the course entitled 'Healing our Relationship with God'. Feathers are always ruffled as we examine our false religions conditioning and misperceptions. This session aims to release any old spiritual wounds that may be in the way. It never fails to set our spirituality onto a stronger and truer footing. It is a huge relief to let out feelings of anger, abandonment, injustice, fear and guilt from our religious past in an open and accepting environment. I am always stunned by the power of the breakthroughs that occur. I will never forget one of these sessions where a wonderful Brazilian woman in the group let out in true Latin style: 'God, where the f**k are you? Get down here where I can see you. You've got no *cohannas!*' ('Balls' to you and I.) After discharging her grievances around God's apparent absence and injustice, her spiritual life took on a new richness and maturity.

Connect with your feelings about God now

Sit somewhere quiet, close your eyes, and just say to yourself the word GOD – GOD – GOD, over and over in your mind. For the purpose of this exercise, do not choose a less charged name. Focus entirely on your feeling response. Remember to breathe and be willing not to judge yourself for anything that you feel.

⬤ Notice the sensations in your body and what emotions, memories and thoughts arise. Breathe and allow them all. Treat every feeling as helpful information to bring you closer to your goal. Write down your feelings and, if possible, share them with a friend.

⬤ To take this one step further, you may wish to go to a church or temple as close as possible to your family denomination. Sit at the back and simply breathe and notice your feelings. Feel whatever is there; be it anger, sadness, anxiety or frustration. There are no 'wrong' or 'bad' feelings. Feelings only want to be felt in the spirit of non-resistance. Do this and they will soon ease. Re-commit to the relationship with God that you would like to have.

Fearful spiritual skeletons left unhealed in your closet, like fearful indoctrination, cruelty from a spiritual authority figure or even just conditioned negative beliefs about God, can create a subtle psychological platform of a force in the universe that does not entirely accept and support you.

Consciously or unconsciously, if your deepest perception of God is fearful, judgemental, conditional or punishing, you will tend to be judgemental, conditional, punishing and fearful with yourself. However you see and treat yourself at core will be how others see and treat you.

With fear, judgement, punishment and conditions dominant within your psyche, automatically you will attract others who reflect this back to you. You will return the favour, treating others in the way that reflects your sense of self. Your primal relationship to your God determines how you think of yourself. Unconsciously, you then project this dynamic onto everyone and everything. Holding onto a fearful image of God is not a good recipe for a happy and peaceful life.

Your relationship to your God is the most intimate mirror you have. It is therefore the most powerful force for positive transformation. Your fundamental sense of self is wrapped up in this relationship. Essentially, your God = yourself = your life. Your core dynamic with God ripples outwards to influence every aspect of your life.

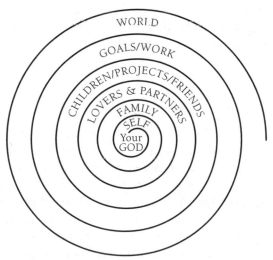

Your relationship dynamics reveal all

Years of counselling people through their greatest difficulties have led me to the conclusion that the primary issues we have with the core people in our life mirror the same issues we have with God. Reflect upon the primary complaints you have about your parents or partners. This will mirror your unconscious perceptions of God. It will also give you a whole new insight into the healing of your human relationships. Heal your dynamic with God, your most central relationship, and you open up a whole new possibility for all your relationships. Has the primary difficulty in your human relationships been of:

* **Abandonment?** 'They were never really available/ there for me', or 'They left me.'
* **Rejection?** 'They didn't want me', or 'I wasn't what they wanted', or 'They don't care.'
* **Condemnation?** 'No matter how hard I try, I cannot be good enough for them.'
* **Difficulty in receiving?** 'I don't deserve this much love', or 'I feel guilty about how much they gave.'

Whatever your recurring bottom line, assume that the difficulties you have about the significant people in your life are really a projection of the complaints you have towards God. At the deepest level, everything going on in your life reflects your dance with God. Anything other than love is simply a misunderstanding that you can ask for Divine help with. Again, re-commit to the relationship with God (and others) that you would like to have.

Write an unedited 'Dear God' letter

Now that you have gained greater awareness of your unhelpful spiritual conditioning, apply the following healing balm. Begin by having some sheets of blank paper and writing materials before you.

Close your eyes for a moment as you contemplate your feelings towards God, reflecting upon the awareness you have gained through the previous exercises. When you are ready, write at the top of the page 'Dear God,' and then be willing to pour your deepest feelings, yearnings and dreams out onto the page. It is important that you write whatever comes. Just focus on watching your hand move across the paper without concern for whether or not your content makes sense or is 'appropriate'. This is not meant to be a polite letter, but an avenue for you to express yourself as nakedly as you can.

Whenever I find myself really stuck emotionally, writing a 'Dear God' letter never fails to purge my fear and lift me to greater clarity.

A healing meditation

Sit somewhere quiet and comfortable with your letter to God and your written spiritual goal before you.

Close your eyes and turn your focus within. Breathe and feel your feelings without trying to force or change anything. Breathe and let your body, mind and whole being soften and quieten . . . .

Feel a sense of falling inwards towards the deepest recesses of your heart, as though a loving, supportive presence effortlessly draws you there.

Begin to see the presence of a wise and tender being approaching you . . . an inner guide of immense light who emanates total love and acceptance of you . . . . It may take the form of a recognisable figure such as Jesus, Buddha, the Holy Mother, a luminous angel, or someone from your past whom you felt unconditionally loved by. They are here to help facilitate your release. They walk towards you now with open arms.

As this guide draws closer, let yourself fall into its loving arms. Rest in an embrace of profound understanding, allowing yourself to be held with all of your yearnings for a truer spirituality.

In your mind's eye, give to your inner guide everything that holds you back from your spiritual intention . . . . Give over each difficulty you have had with God, as though handing over a series of dark shadows . . . perhaps the sting of religious authority figures who once imposed their fearful viewpoints onto you . . . the times you've felt let down, abandoned, alone, heart broken over God's apparent lack of response to your needs . . . .

Hand to this being whatever stands between you joyously walking towards the Boundless Love of God and your essence. Feel how much love you are offered in the face of every difficulty . . . how deeply you are listened to . . . how present love is to you.

_⊘_ Notice how each difficulty you give over evaporates into nothing in the hands of this guide . . . leaving you lighter and freer. Let every difficulty, every painful past memory, be given over and dissolved into light, until your internal slate is clear.

_⊘_ Ask your inner guide to lead you into a deeper experience of your true relationship with God. See yourself being led by this guide into a field ablaze with the most brilliant light . . . . Stand in the centre of this field and be willing to receive anew . . . receive Boundless Love, boundless blessings, boundless peace.

_⊘_ Let your heart rest in the limitless peace of your true relationship with God . . . . Offer your thanks for what you have received . . . ask for any help you feel you may need . . . and when you are ready bring your focus to the place where you are sitting. Take a few deeper breaths, take a stretch and slowly open your eyes.

No matter what you may have been taught about God, through these exercises you will come to realise that an experience of Boundless Love is all that awaits you. In this awareness you will see that God never wanders from you. Sewn into the fabric of your existence, God could never abandon you. However many times you may forget and wander from your Divine heritage, you can return to it whenever you want.

'Now, why not consider a lasting truce with yourself and God?'

Hafiz

Part II

INNER
WISDOM

4

Remember who you are

'Try to identify with the
part of your mind
where stillness and peace
reign forever.'

A Course in Miracles

On our first visit to India, Robert and I visited many ashrams, temples, mosques, churches and teachers. Our romantic dreams of sitting at the feet of saints were initially shattered by schemes of trickster priests whose goal was to extract large sums of money from our pockets. They threatened 'bad karma' if we refused. They spoke vehemently at us about their particular teaching being the only way. It was tiresome and irritating. We soon realised that the spiritual invitation under our nose was to stop seeking without and turn our focus to the jewels within. This we did: and our pilgrimage became positively life changing.

Having stopped seeking, something prompted us to join friends we met on the road to visit their teacher's ashram. I was weak and light-headed from a bad dose of dysentery. A playful four-year old boy greeted us in the ashram's inner sanctums. Laughing, he ran to me, grabbed hold of my legs, looked up and said, 'Who are you?' Assuming he was asking me to introduce myself, I replied, 'I am Miranda.' He laughed hysterically as though hearing the world's funniest joke, and repeated his question, 'No, who are you?' Again I repeated my answer. Again he laughed, and asked for the third time, 'No, who are you?'

Call me slow (I blame it on the dysentery) but the third time I got the message and dissolved into laughter with him. This four-year old boy, son of the Mataji (holy mother) of the ashram, was playfully prompting me to loosen my attachment to my ego sense of self. I was reminded to identify more with the eternal self that is beyond name, limits, culture and age, and exists as a cell within the Boundless. I see it as no accident that the meeting we then had with the 'mother' of the ashram opened me into a state of profound bliss. Laughing and loosening my attachment to my ego self made me more receptive to a truer awareness.

The goal of all mystic paths is to release you into your Boundless Self; to unfurl who you think you are, revealing who you truly are. Who you think you are at core shapes your life. I'm not talking about your superficial identity built on your age, your race, your gender and your occupation, but your fundamental sense of Self. The path of Jnanni yoga – the yoga of wisdom exemplified by the great Hindu saints Krishnamurti and Ramana Maharshi – directs aspirants over a lifetime to deeply contemplate the question 'Who am I?' Within this question is the key to existence.

Who you think you are determines every decision you make and everything that you experience. Who you think you are unconsciously determines what you believe you deserve, and therefore how much happiness, success, love, ease, grace and goodness you can have. Who you think you are determines how you think, how you feel, what you see, what you gravitate towards and what gravitates towards you. Few people see themselves accurately. Cleave to your true identity.

'You are the light of the world'
(New Testament)

Jesus did not say, 'Some of you are the light of the world.' He said you, plural. Jesus did not lay conditions or get-out clauses upon being the light of the world. He did not say you are the light of the world if you have never made a mistake, if you have no attachments, if you never lose your temper, if you are good and kind to everyone all of the time. He simply said, 'You are the light of the world.' Furthermore, passages within the Hebrew scriptures say, 'Ye are gods, children of the most high, all of you.'

The Hindu *Upanishads* say, 'There is a light that shines beyond all things, beyond the heavens, the very highest heavens. It is the light that shines within your heart.' They cannot all be wrong.

You are the light of the world because you are the presence of Boundless Love on earth. Considering yourself thus does not make you arrogant, conceited or superior to others because everyone else is the light of the world along with you. Accepting this draws from you a profound humility and reverence for the sacredness of being alive.

You are here on this earth to shine the light of eternity. You do this every time you remember the truth of your Self and offer your love. The form that takes ultimately is irrelevant. Remembering who you are supports you in fulfilling your unique soul purpose: giving your gifts to bless others. Imagine registering that you really are the light of the world. How would that impact the way you think, feel and live?

Most days I am privileged to sit with people sharing the parts of themselves they rarely show anyone. Although my clients may believe these aspects of self are unacceptable, weak or flawed, all I see in their moments of vulnerability is indescribable beauty. Whenever anyone lets go of their outer mask all that remains is God. I feel like reaching into their heart and showing them their own divinity. The moments I manage to do this are the times of the greatest grace for me.

If only you could see how beautiful you are. The idea that you could possibly be inadequate, ugly or incomplete would have you in hysterical laughter. No matter what you have been through in life, your essence is boundless and holy. Connected with infinity, your true self has power to reverse the laws of the world, being beyond the restriction of time, space, distance and limit of any kind.

Look beneath your mask

I will let you in on a cosmic secret: underneath the masks we all wear, everyone feels lacking or flawed to some degree. It is part of the primary human condition I will outline more in the next chapter. Typically, you fear to investigate these feelings too closely lest you become overwhelmed and lose the ability to appear that you have it all together. You fail to realise that your defences, masks and coping strategies keep the illusory vision of yourself alive. This keeps you away from Boundless Love. Every veil of defence you let drop takes you closer to who you really are, and to greater freedom and happiness.

In the Zen tradition, koans or riddles are contemplated in meditation to help interrupt illusions and open the student to truer states. One of the most famous is the question, 'What was your original face before you were born?' Using this koan to explore the theme of identity at an Interfaith Seminary class, Jenny, an intelligent, articulate and brilliant professional in her late thirties went into deep fear.

Jenny was terrified of exploring her original face, which she had assumed was scarred, repulsive even. Deep down, she believed that to uncover what she related to as her essence would reveal something so ugly and unlovable it would cause others to reject her once and for all. With gentle encouragement, Jenny managed to step through her fear. To her delight she began to feel whole for the first time in her life.

Prior to this moment Jenny had spent years in therapy trying to cope with a sense of herself as internally scarred, re-viewing events in her childhood that confirmed her perception of herself. She had never paused to ask herself the question, 'Is this vision of myself actually true?' Jenny discovered that it wasn't. In facing your worst fears, you would too.

Somewhere along the line you have absorbed a vision of yourself that contradicts who you are. Psychology points to childhood conditioning received through your parents, environment and culture. Although these influences have a profound impact, the birth of your separate, limited identity did not begin there. On a soul level, it began the moment you first experienced yourself as separate from your Source.

This first experience of feeling separate, which can occur before, during or after our birth, is metaphorically the original sin (mistake), which seemingly expelled us out of the Garden of Eden (connection to Boundless Love). Childhood events and adult traumas then serve to anchor our sense of separation, acting out our sense of incompleteness with others. The notion of separation and duality rules this world, but it cannot change reality.

I have learned that whatever your personal history, the truth of who you are remains intact. As a diamond is still a diamond even when it is hidden under dirt, so underneath your fears and seeming human imperfections, your essence remains as God created it: intact and still whole. The worst that can happen is that the diamond within you can be buried under so much dust that you forget that there was ever a diamond within at all. Even so, it doesn't alter the diamond. Your essence can never be destroyed.

Excavate your inherent perfection

Your spirituality will serve either to help free you from your mistaken self-concepts or it will subtly reinforce them by deepening the notion that you must 'become' perfect through endless prayers, meditations and practices. The intention you give your spirituality will determine where it takes you. Direct your spirituality not to *becoming* something different, but to *unwinding* what you have assimilated that is false.

You do not need to work to create the perfect self. It exists already as the Boundless Love within you. You cannot top that. Focus instead on letting go of everything else. Look to your defences. If you were to let go of the strategies you think you need to keep safe, what do you fear would be exposed? In letting your fears of who you are come up for air, you will realise that in truth they are nothing.

In the second year of the Interfaith Seminary training, we guide participants through a powerful exercise in pairs to recover a truer sense of identity. Sitting opposite one another, one person asks the other the question, 'Who are you?' over and over again for 30 minutes. The questioner says nothing else. Initially, participants grapple with their self-concepts, trying to answer the question logically. Eventually, they let go of their own answers and come to a place of not knowing. The attempt to even speak falls away. Still being asked, 'Who are you?' they drop into a deeper knowing of the truth of their being, often accompanied by gentle laughter and tender tears of release.

Recover a truer sense of identity: a meditation

I suggest you do this meditation either with a friend you trust, by looking at your own reflection in a mirror or by simply reflecting in silence. Decide on how long you will meditate (at least 10 minutes) and commit to this length of time.

_✐_ Firstly, set your intention. Sit with the prayer, 'Take me into a truer experience of my Self', until you feel sincere in your request.

_✐_ When ready, begin asking yourself gently, 'Who am I?' (If working with a friend, have them begin gently asking, 'Who are you?')

_✐_ Keep asking the question, or having it asked of you. Let it take you beyond your self-concepts into something truer. Let the question take you into a place of pure being.

Grace will reveal to you something of your own beauty.
That will shed light on everything.

5

One problem:
one solution

Let us make all spiritual talk simple:
All problems arise from wandering into separation and fear.
All solutions begin by returning to the Boundless Love within.

In my private practice, retreats and groups, I have worked with thousands of people over the years. Each person seemed to suffer from distinctly different problems: relationship heartbreaks, difficult family dynamics, divorce, trauma, bereavement, sickness, depression, addictions, financial and work stress. Although individuals and situations are unique, the approach I take with everyone is fundamentally the same: identifying and letting go of fearful beliefs, to help them return to their centre within Boundless Love again. Every lasting change begins from within.

I have come to see that whatever you are currently facing in life, there is only one central conflict. You have wandered from your Source, forgotten who you are, and have fallen into a way of being that cuts you off from your true strength, vision and purpose. This causes life to unfold in a way that is often painful, difficult and frightening. There is a simple solution. No matter how far you wander from God and your true Self, you can return to it in any moment. When you are at peace within, you can see clearly what needs to be approached differently.

To make lasting, substantial changes in your circumstances, first change your consciousness. It is very human to think that if your outer circumstances would change – if your partner would be more loving and attentive of you, your children less demanding, your work situation were different, you had a different family, a better bank balance, possessed the looks of a super-model and the brain of a genius – all would be well. Almost everyone has been raised to believe that problems are 'out there'. Yet your only essential problem is that you think yourself separate and alone and have assimilated a fearful way of being that dissociates you from who you are.

This tiny mistake in identity causes endless havoc and complications in your life. It disconnects you from your natural wisdom. Peace and clarity shine when you return to the awareness of your heritage in Boundless Love. The practical way forward becomes obvious. Return to your centre and outer problems either dissolve or you find yourself at a place of serenity within them.

I have found it immensely helpful to understand our two fundamental states of being. Although reality is non-dual in nature, to be human is to experience dual states: a higher self and a lower self. Each 'self' gives rise to a completely different 'reality'. Every mystic tradition has spoken of these two inner realities by a different name. Christians called it the Christ self and the Devil, Buddhists your Buddha nature and the ego, Hindus the atman and the ego. I will call this your Boundless Self and your Ego Self. The goal is to ground yourself more deeply in your Boundless Self and learn to witness your Ego Self. The more you learn to do this, the happier and more effortless your life will become. Enlightenment is the moment when you let the fearful, separate ego state fall away altogether.

Boundless reality

Your Boundless Self is grounded in the principle of unity. Knowing that you are the extension of God, in this state you feel intimately connected to everyone and everything. Your Boundless Self naturally thinks through the pathways of love, peace and inherent innocence. When grounded in your Boundless Self, fear, guilt and lack do not even figure, and you live in the present moment.

In this, your natural state of being, you feel loved, whole, accepted, free, clear, at ease, happy and at home. You relate to others and the world harmoniously. Appreciation, gratitude and kindness come naturally. Identifying with unity and love, all good things generate. Happiness, creativity, free self-expression and a compassionate instinct to serve others flow effortlessly. Centred in the clarity of your Boundless Self, life is wonderfully simple.

Think of three occasions you have experienced being in your Boundless Self. Times when you have felt deeply happy, fulfilled, at peace, at one, innocent and connected. Ask yourself:

What was I doing right?

Ego 'realities'

Your Ego Self is grounded in the illusion of separation and alone-ness. This state is fathered in the forgetting of your divinity and mothered by the conditioning of this world. It causes you to see yourself as a body independent from God and disconnected from others. Now feeling very small and alone in the universe, a mind-set of fear, guilt and lack is born. You begin to feel there is some-thing wrong with you, and a negative script emerges to try to make sense of why you feel incomplete. Your ego script is a neg-ative judgement about yourself. It can take many forms and some common scripts include:

* 'I'm not good enough.'
* 'I'm nothing.'
* 'I'm bad.'
* 'I'm wrong.'
* 'I'm worthless.'

To your Boundless Self, these verdicts are absurd lies, but to your Ego Self they are the foundation of your being. They keep you locked into the past and afraid of the future. Pushed deep into the sub-conscious mind, they are the source of all that is difficult in your life. To see them clearly is to begin loosening their hold over you.

Identifying your illusions gives you greater freedom from them. Whether your psychic pain occurs in the area of your relationships, your work, your family, your health or elsewhere, the underlying cause of your suffering is your mistaken sense of Self. Your spiritu-ality can help loosen your attachment to it. Seeing illusions clearly gives you the capacity to witness them without condemnation. This helps you avoid getting caught up in unnecessary drama. The first step is to identify how the ego grounds itself in you.

Uncovering your ego script

Sit somewhere quiet and comfortable.

⤶ Ask for Divine help to surround and support you, providing a feeling of love and safety. Remind yourself that truth opens the doorway to a new level of freedom. Call to mind a persistent problem you have. Perhaps it is a recurring dynamic in a relationship, a sense of limitation, a frustration you hit in your more difficult moments that causes you to feel negative about yourself, others and life.

⤶ Allow yourself to feel into that in as much detail as possible. Then ask yourself: 'When [name of someone you have difficulty with] does [whatever it is that upsets you], I wind up feeling 'I'm . . . .' 'When [limitation or difficulty] happens, I feel that I'm . . . .' A repeated experience of rejection, for example, is a pattern and not the actual verdict.

⤶ Go underneath it by asking, '[Name] rejects/judges/overlooks me because I'm . . . .' Go through your various areas of upset with these questions and listen for the common theme. 'The bottom line most negative verdict I have about myself is . . . .'

⤶ Your Ego Self's negative verdict will always begin with, 'I'm . . . .' It is an inner put-down that will leave you feeling small, inadequate, hopeless and disempowered. It keeps you unnecessarily bound.

Projection renders you powerless

Ever since Adam blamed Eve for listening to the serpent, the Ego Self has been projecting the blame for your bad feelings onto someone or something else. The Ego Self searches for a 'bad guy' to pin the blame onto – anything to divert us from taking responsibility for being creator of our experience. Classically we blame our parents, school, society, partners, children, work colleagues for what they gave us that was difficult, or for what we wanted but they failed to deliver. Underneath all this, we blame God. Blaming always backfires. Additionally, it renders us a victim.

Like scratching a persistent itch, blaming someone else for our pain gives temporary relief, but invariably deepens our sense of hopelessness. Have you ever 'shot off' at someone you love in anger, building a 'justified' case against them and letting them bear the brunt of your rage? Have you ever noticed that although this gave you momentary release, it didn't resolve anything, only left you feeling like a nasty person? Human beings are not separate but intimately connected to one another. The Buddha said, 'Everything you give you give to yourself.' Every time you project and dump, you wind up embedding your ego's negative verdict about yourself further. Blaming hides your wound underground and takes you further from the solution.

Defences fail to protect you

After judging yourself as not good enough, bad, wrong, nothing or worthless, and then projecting the blame onto someone or something outside yourself, your Ego Self builds up defence systems to protect itself against future hurt. This misguided attempt to keep safe only deepens your pain, and gives further 'weight' to your script. Defences cause you to enter into difficult dynamics with others. Other people become like actors on a stage called 'your life' acting out your beliefs for you. The extent to which you are unconscious of your ego's script, other people and the world will play it out. This can make your life into a cheap drama, keeping struggle and stress going. To your Boundless Self it is an invitation to gain awareness of your illusions and rise to a truer reality.

A client called Jonathan was an ambitious and highly gifted writer in his forties. A sensitive soul acting as a high achiever, he never felt acknowledged. Socially his wife would always seem the focus of their families' and friends' interests, even though he was a fascinating and likeable man. Jonathan often felt left out, negated and unimportant. Internally accusing others of treating him as though he wasn't there, he felt painfully separate from his wife, family and friends whom he loved. Constantly trying harder for people to like and acknowledge him, nothing he did seemed to work. One day he walked into our session really angry. It was clear to me that his anger masked deep grief at feeling he didn't matter. His unconscious negative verdict about himself was 'I'm nothing'.

Externally confident, Jonathan felt deeply alone. I suggested we face this. When he made contact with his sense of 'nothingness' Jonathan began to see things very differently. He recognised that his wife's popularity was not to blame for his feelings, neither was the behaviour of his friends and family. He even saw painful childhood events that resulted in feeling left out and unimportant as his ego script's set-up. Jonathan saw painful life events as other people acting out his negative script about himself on the stage of life. He acknowledged that the real cause of his heartache was his own false belief, and that this belief was just a mistake that he had the power to let go of.

I taught Jonathan to treat his need for acknowledgement with kindness, witnessing without judgement his ego script of 'I'm nothing', and to ask for Divine help in re-centring back to his Boundless Self. He began praying for help in forgiving those who had played out his negative script for him in the past, and in forgiving himself for believing it. Each day in meditation he surrendered this painful verdict of himself to God.

Within weeks, Jonathan was staggered at how profoundly the world seemed to change around his new inner state. People began paying him more attention and consideration. Without any external trying, Jonathan had gained a more genuine inner confidence, felt more lovingly connected to his wife, friends and family, and gained a new peace of mind.

Witness and return to centre

No matter how deeply embedded your mind is in ego awareness and how messy your life, within you exists a psychic bridge to eternity. This bridge becomes apparent through your willingness. Whenever you do not feel at peace, know you have slipped into identifying with your Ego Self and its illusions of separation, fear, guilt and lack, which leads you down the slippery slope of blame, projection, attack and defensiveness. You will know when you are there because life will feel a struggle. Here's what to do:

* **Stop** trying to fix the outer situation for a moment. Just witness what is happening within you.
* **Name** what you are feeling inwardly without judging it as good or bad: 'anger', 'disappointment', 'hurt', 'nervous', 'insecure', 'uncertain', 'sad', 'distracted', etc.
* **Breathe**. Be present and kind to yourself in these feelings. Do

not try to exterminate them, but do not try to act them out. Just feel what's there.
* **Recognise** that the core problem is not in the situation, but in your forgetting of your true self. This has disconnected you from your natural wisdom and the true way forward.
* **Be willing** to return to your centre within Boundless Love.
* **Ask** for Divine help in letting go of your ego verdicts, stories and blame games. Pray, 'Anchor me back to my Boundless Self.'
* **Allow** peace to come to you.

You are not alone

You are not supposed to do life on your own. Let the Boundless help you. Let other people help you. God's grace will respond fully to your slightest invitation. Divine help comes through your willingness not through effort. You have been programmed for a wonderful life, but this will only come if you are willing to become more appropriately dependent upon the Boundless. How can you expect to move beyond ego awareness if your Ego Self is directing the process?

Personally, I regularly dance back and forth across the bridge from my Ego Self to my Boundless Self. However, the experience of unity, joy, flow and peace are much more predominant than they have ever been. My ego scripts drive me significantly less. In many areas of my life, I have ceased to play them out altogether. I notice much more quickly when I have slipped into separation and fear, and therefore am able to return to centre more quickly. This has dramatically reduced the amount of time I spend being unhappy.

Although we release our attachment to our ego identities piece by piece, there inevitably will come a time when we register the ego for what it truly is; merely a speck of dust in the scheme of the cosmos. Then we will laugh, as many enlightened ones before us have laughed. We will know that all that has troubled us, tripped us up, caused so many heartaches, has had absolutely zero impact in reality, and is nothing at all.

'The truth in you remains as radiant as a star, as pure as light, as innocent as love itself.'
A Course in Miracles

6

Dialling direct to God

'God is nearer to you
Than your own jugular vein'
Sri Ramakrishna

At the age of 21 I left Australia on a one-way ticket to England. I arrived on Easter Sunday with everything I owned in two suitcases, no plans, and money to last only a few months. It made no rational sense. In Australia I was onto a good thing. During the day I taught meditation and stress management. In the evenings I presented the news and weather at the local television station. I had good friends, bright prospects and an interesting life. Although my feet were itchy, England was way down on my list. But one morning I woke up knowing in every cell of my being that I needed to leave everything and begin a new life in England. It was beyond logic – something I just had to do.

The guidance was so strong, more like a Divine order than intuition. I do not remember feeling afraid or apprehensive, despite being alone in a new country and not knowing anyone. My trust seemed to be rewarded by many extraordinary synchronicities unfolding effortlessly. Within eight weeks of arrival I had a home, a thriving spiritual counselling practice and a few friends to my name. Nine months later I met my husband Robert on a television talk show titled *The time: The place*. There is no way I could have hatched such a brilliant plan. I landed on my feet in a major level of flow. The months and years that followed seemed intricately orchestrated to provide the maximum personal and spiritual growth in the shortest possible time. Following this guidance was the smartest thing I ever did.

I have come to see that God understands my best interests

more clearly than I do. Whenever I centre in the Boundless Love of God and my true Self, and intimately invite it to lead my decision-making, life flows effortlessly. Trying to work life out on my own is nowhere near as successful. Listening to higher wisdom makes for a wonderful life.

Most of your sufferings come from believing that you know better than God. You were not designed to be independent of your Source. The vision of your Ego Self is extremely narrow, your knowledge of the larger plan limited. The Boundless is whispering messages of love, remembrance and wisdom to you in every encounter, sight, sound and most of all in the deep silence. Learning to listen, trust in and discern genuine inspiration from subtle egoism gives you mighty wings with which to fly more effortlessly through life.

Some years ago I wondered whether it were possible to progress from having occasional flashes of intuition and synchronicity to ongoing inspirational dialogue. I began to explore the idea of accessing a pure level of inner guidance every day. I discovered that within everyone lives a voice for God, an inner teacher whose wisdom can be drawn upon at any time. I have shared my discoveries and methods on guidance with many people who have found them transforming and deeply practical.

Accessing higher wisdom means you do not have to struggle to figure out difficult issues on your own. Inspiration can come to answer questions and problems, accompanied by new levels of energy with which to move forward. Genuine guidance helps you to live life on purpose.

Go direct

In the western world we are seeing a mass turning away from religious intermediaries to seek God through direct experience. This approach is emphasised in the Zen proverb, 'Seek not to follow in the footsteps of masters; rather, seek what they sought.' Although a teacher is invaluable to inspire you, point the way and help illuminate your obstacles, no one can walk the path on your behalf. Your soul's yearning for liberation, homecoming, deep peace, joy, unity and love can only be met by direct experience. If you are hungry, someone else eating does not ease your hunger. If you are tired, someone else resting will not relieve your weariness. If you seek to know God, someone else's awakening will not awaken you.

In the past, the idea of directly accessing Divine wisdom has been regarded either as blasphemy or a certain route to delusion. In truth, there is never a moment when God is not speaking to you. The Divine gives fully and freely to all, having no favourites. God is speaking to you right now. Attune yourself that you may receive the answers to your deepest questions and yearnings. Levels of knowing, deep peace and timeless wisdom can be yours.

Learning to hear Divine guidance is synonymous with releasing the illusion of your self as separate. Just as children automatically inherit the DNA structure of their physical parents, as a child of God you are naturally imbued with the qualities and attributes of your Creator. Recognising your oneness with your Boundless Source, you remember that you too are Boundless. That means nothing is beyond you. You can hear the voice of God because of who you are. When you identify yourself as Boundless Love, you recognise that there is no lack of wisdom, clarity, peace or joy. Whenever you open your mind beyond the illusory boundaries of separation, hearing Divine guidance becomes quite natural. Returning back into your natural state, guidance becomes an act of receiving what is already given.

Join your mind with God

Sit quietly. Focus on breathing evenly and relaxing your physical body. Take what time you need to calm your senses.

Imagine stepping back from the image of yourself as a separate body. Ask, 'Help me connect with my Boundless Self who is One within God.' Do not force anything, just breathe and welcome a truer awareness.

'Ask and you shall Receive' (New Testament)

It has come apparent to me in my years of exploring the depths of the human psyche that our Ego Self fundamentally wants to BE God: that is where our cherished notion of independence comes from. Although a level of practical self-sufficiency is essential in order to handle adult life, spiritual independence is disastrous. The unconscious insistence on doing everything yourself blocks you from asking for and receiving Divine help. This keeps you in control but is extremely limited.

In my experience, in order to receive you must ask. Here's why. Although there is never an instant when grace is absent, the Boundless always offers freedom, and will never violate your choice to be self-sufficient. When you do not ask for guidance, wisdom or assistance, essentially your communication is, 'I can handle this on my own thank you.' God will never come uninvited: that would be tantamount to spiritual burglary. Whenever you ask for the awareness of the Boundless presence, the grace that has always been there in the background becomes active. This is why prayer is so powerful. Prayer is asking for that which has already been given to come to the forefront of your awareness. We will explore this in more detail later.

Many people are unused to asking and have become too proficient in thinking that they either should know all the answers already or that they are a failure if they are unable to figure it out on their own. Other blocks to asking include feeling unable to ask, believing you don't deserve to ask, feeling guilty about asking or not knowing how to ask. Perhaps you need to ask for help in learning to ask for help! It really is OK to do this. The Hindu avatar Mother Meera has said many times, 'You ask for far too little. Ask for everything.'

What to ask for?

If you ask for material things you may well get them, but will probably not feel the fulfilment you expected them to bring. It is better to move from asking for things you believe would make you happy to asking to be re-aligned with the source of all happiness. In this you discover that everything you truly want is already present.

When you ask for help in letting go of your own limitations that obscure the truth so that you may return into alignment, you will be answered with a deep peace. Within this you will find that God IS, Truth IS, You ARE. In such a level of alignment, words become meaningless.

In focusing on the real issue – the healing and raising of your consciousness – you can begin asking for help with letting go of the blocks to knowing and living from Boundless Love. Through your prayers, give to the Divine your attachment to any patterns, beliefs or thoughts blocking your way to receiving direct guidance. For example:

Beloved God, I give to You my attachment
to the belief that I am not good enough to receive.
Help me let this go and open to the
Truth of Who I really am.
Amen.

Beloved God, I release to You my belief
that I am separate and alone.
Help me feel and know that Your Boundless Love
is with me, guiding me always.
Amen.

Having grounded yourself in the truth of your Boundless Self within God, there is nothing to stop you from simply turning within, dropping into the quiet place of the heart and asking whatever you want help with. It is that simple, yet takes much courage. Towards the end of my morning practice spent stilling my mind, I consciously invite God to come to me. Sufis would call this, 'Welcoming the Friend.' Once I feel a greater sense of calm I begin to ask the following questions and sit listening to what comes. Sit quietly with these questions. Expect a response.

1 What would You have me receive?

The response I receive to this is always a feeling of immense, indescribable love, a reservoir of infinite peace, unity and expansion, which is sometimes accompanied by the word of a particular quality. Put all your expectations aside and be open. Sense yourself as light sitting within a beam of light, letting whatever it is you truly need wash over you. Allow yourself to be re-infused.

2 What would You have me know?

The answers I receive to this are always simple, direct and relate to how I see myself, other people and the world. Do not overlook the simple answers you receive to this question – they are usually the most profound.

3 What would You have me let go of?

All obstacles are attachments to something illusory that you have invested in as real and necessary. The responses I receive to this question are usually incisive and shown to me with great compassion. (If there is any sense of condemnation accompanying this response you can be sure that is coming from your own ego.)

4 What would You have me do?

Asking this question supports me in letting my actions be guided by the higher will, not my own egocentric desires. God's plan for your day will always be more joyous and successful than yours.

If you have a specific issue you need guidance on, ask: 'In relation to [a particular concern, relationship or issue] . . . what would You have me receive/know/look at and let go of/do?' Use this as the basis for further dialogue until you are clear. Sometimes words come, sometimes images – but, above all, there is always a feeling of deep peace and love.

God speaks your language

One thing is certain: if you align yourself and ask with sincerity, you will get a response, only do not get attached to the form of how you should receive guidance. You may not even get 'answers' within your meditation, but instead may pick up a book or hear someone's words that resonate and address your questions. Some people are highly visual, and see prolific images and pictures that point the way for them. Others have an auditory dominance and are likely to hear a 'voice' telling them what they need to know. Others are primarily kinaesthetic in that they receive guidance through emotional feelings and physical sensations. You may wake up one morning just 'knowing' the answer. Every person is unique and will receive answers in a way that is most personally meaningful to them. Don't worry: the Boundless knows how you tick.

Try not to compare your experience with another's. The real point is that your dialogue brings you to peace. If you make it your habit to ask and listen sincerely, you will become accustomed to receiving answers. God will appear in the form of a love that fills your heart. Never doubt that.

'Know that God is with you now,
as fully and as totally as you experience yourself.'

Tom Carpenter

Opening up to inspiration

'Where do you think you will be
When God reveals Himself
Inside you?'

Hafiz

Two young women, Leah and Emka, both university students,
attended a weekend workshop I facilitated called *Walking your
true spiritual path*. Among other things I introduced them to
the method for accessing guidance that I shared with you in
the previous chapter. A fortnight later, Emka was in crisis.
Committed to leaving the university halls of residence the
following week, she and her boyfriend had not found anywhere
to live on their tiny budget.

Having exhausted every conceivable option, Leah suggested
they go into meditation together and ask for guidance. As soon
as they asked, 'What would You have me receive?' the communal
telephone situated immediately outside their door began to
ring. While they spent the next half an hour asking within for
guidance, the telephone rang its full course three times without
being answered. They assumed that to do so would be resistance
to the inner listening process.

After the meditation they were still none the wiser. Checking
her email later that day, Emka opened a message from her
boyfriend saying, 'Where were you today? I called and called to
tell you that I've found somewhere wonderful for us to live. I
can't wait for you to see it!'

I have discovered that my single greatest obstacle to receiving
guidance is the expectation I have to its coming. Any genuine
prayer of the heart is answered instantaneously, however the
answer may take a different shape to the one you expect. Rarely

will it be like a loudspeaker in your ear saying, 'Hello, this is God here. The answer is ....' Suspend your expectations of how you believe inspiration will come to you. If you pay attention it will come in the way you can best hear. Leah and Emka did well to turn within, align themselves with the Boundless and ask for help. Their request was answered in the most immediate form. They just forgot to listen to the obvious. Receiving guidance is an act of deep listening.

What blocks guidance?

Ease and flow are the natural order of things. A Biblical psalm says, 'It is your Father's good pleasure to give your the Kingdom.' There is absolutely no need for you to struggle because life really is abundant. However, there have been many occasions when I have felt stuck and unable to gain the clarity I need for the way forward. In retrospect I recognise in these moments I had blocked the flow of inspiration by falling out of alignment with my Boundless Self. Moving into an ego state of fear and separation made Divine help feel far away. Recentring in a more truthful state of being always manages to bring me back into the flow of inner wisdom.

If you are asking and feel you are not receiving, do not be despondent. Simply be willing to look more honestly at what prevents you from receiving the clarity you need. Here are some of the obstacles most likely to pull you out of alignment.

Thoughts of separation

Notice how every fear, anxiety, stress or negative feeling is rooted in the thought that you are alone and separate in this world. Separation makes you feel frail and lacking. It makes inspiration feel far away. Whenever I let go of seeing myself as separate and instead remember my boundlessness within God, I immediately notice a greater receptivity. Be willing daily to give up the thought that you are separate from God and from others. This is singularly one of the most powerful things you can do.

Thoughts of judgement

Judgement in any form is a contrary force to the way of love. Judgement blocks inspired wisdom, which sees the bigger picture without condemnation. Your judgements are always a projection of your self-judgement. They anchor your sense of separation and leave you feeling bad about yourself. No matter how seemingly justified, holding judgements always directs your awareness away from the wisdom of your Boundless Self. I notice that whenever I loosen my attachment to judgements a higher vision takes its place.

Thoughts of guilt and anger

Guilt is a distorted viewpoint. Justifying or holding onto guilt is the fastest way to drain your energy and pull you out of alignment with the Boundless. Everyone makes mistakes, but holding yourself or anyone else in guilt does not protect from the same mistakes recurring. Only forgiveness does that. Every time I release thoughts of guilt, be that about myself or someone else, I notice new waves of energy and clarity.

Thoughts of pride and 'special-ness'

Pride is a mask for inadequacy. Both are expressions of spiritual arrogance because they deny who you really are. When opening up your intuition, it is particularly important not to let spiritual gifts become hijacked by the ego for purposes of separation over others. Boundless Love and inspiration are not special to anyone, rather, they are universal. The more I let go of my need to be 'special' or 'better' over another in any way, the clearer I receive guidance. Witness and forgive your need to be a 'spiritual super-star' and the underlying inadequacy it hides.

Trying too hard

Trying too hard blocks you from just letting in the inspiration. Although receiving guidance requires the discipline of regular reflection, hours and hours of spiritual practice a day will not necessarily equal enlightenment. Inspiration occurs through listening not trying. Whenever I find myself 'trying too hard', I notice I am usually facing an unworthiness belief – a feeling that I need to 'earn' the inspiration by lots of hard work. When I re-gain my sense of humour and lighten up a bit, the guidance comes naturally.

Trying to control the guidance

Whenever I am attached to a specific idea or outcome, I am not available for inspiration, but straining to hear what I want to hear. The need to control guidance, a situation or another person is a sure sign that fear is driving. It is better to face your fears and ask for help with them. Then be willing to trust that the Divine plan will take you towards your highest happiness. The best things in life usually occur extra-curricular to your plans. Do not be afraid of the unknown.

Fear of punishment

Deep in the unconscious ego I have noticed a collective belief that we are fundamentally sinful or guilty, and if this were to be exposed we would be severely punished. Thus one of the primary reasons for blocking inspiration, resisting spiritual practice and directing contact with Source is the fear of being destroyed by it. This belief is so unconscious you may not relate to it, but somewhere along the road in your spiritual life, you will. Profound self-compassion will move you forward. Pray, 'Beloved God, let me open to feeling and knowing that in Your eyes I am innocent and deeply loved.'

Fear of 'melt down'

Another primary unconscious fear of direct spiritual contact is that opening to the Boundless would cause you to lose control of your faculties and render you unable to function. In opening more to your Boundless Self, your Ego Self will become less predominant. The more you identify with your ego as who you are, the scarier this feels. Beginning to identify more with the Self that is beyond your personality will help ease your fears. Be courageous. All that can ever melt down are your illusions. The truth in you never changes and never dies.

Ground yourself in Love

Trying to reach for inspiration while holding onto separation, judgement, fear, attachments, guilt, pride and the like, can distort guidance as well as remove you from it. If you do not ground yourself in love, the ego can direct the guidance process to take you into greater states of separation and fear. Boundless Love is the mystic doorway to the highest levels of wisdom and inspiration. Think of the wisest beings you know, and they will invariably also be the most loving.

Opening to hearing, feeling and knowing God more directly is indistinguishable to letting go of your ego identities, beliefs and patterns. The ability to receive clear guidance comes with practice – regular intervals of going within. Just as becoming physically fit takes regular exercise, so toning your inner wisdom muscles may take time and practice. Be patient with yourself. Over time your inner voice will become strong and clear. The more you go within, align yourself, ask and listen, the more you will feel an increasing sense of inner wisdom guiding your daily decision-making and living.

Discerning truth from illusion

Having learnt to listen for guidance, it helps to have some guidelines with which to discern inspired wisdom from your desires. Distinguishing between the voice of your ego and the voice for the Boundless can be subtle. Clearing the blocks to guidance provides a good grounding point, but your own wants and fears can easily hide themselves as the source of the 'inspiration'. The following are the criteria I have evolved for discerning whether the guidance I receive is true or not. Check the inspiration your receive by these five points.

1 If it is true, it is good for all

True guidance is always universally orientated, never harmful. It will always leave you with a feeling of loving kindness towards everyone and will always be a win/win.

2 If it is true, it will feel deeply peaceful and loving

Although true guidance will often stretch you beyond your comfort zones, there will always be an accompanying feeling of deep peace and love.

3 If it is true, it will produce some kind of joining

Love is always orientated towards the principle of unity, the ego towards separation. If your guidance moves you closer towards healing, re-connection, honest communication, forgiveness and integration, you can be confident it is true. Know it is your Ego Self's guidance if it produces a greater sense of isolation, anger, a deepening of righteousness, withdrawal, conflict, guilt and projection.

4 If it is true, it will address your consciousness

True guidance will always work to bring you into a higher state of being. At the highest level, the only corrections needed are at the level of your awareness, for it is from here that all of your actions spring. Sometimes you may get a strong instinct to 'go and do something', which may be fine, but always check your intention for doing it. Many unloving, unkind acts have been done apparently because 'God told me to'. Always check your intention, and trust your instincts, ethics and common sense.

5 If it is true, it can be confirmed

If you are ever in doubt as to whether your guidance is correct, ask for confirmation. This often comes through someone saying exactly the words you were given, through picking up a spiritual book to see the message confirmed there, or events unfolding in a way that clearly responds to your request. In most mystical traditions, confirmation of an inspired message is given three times. Many people find that listening for three confirmations is a sign that the guidance is true.

Over time, the voice for Boundless Love, however you hear, see or feel it, will become unmistakable. You will not fail to recognise its clarity nor question its love. Your choice to begin a sincere Divine dialogue will bring you treasures of profound peace and wisdom. The more you align yourself, ask and listen, the more substantially grace will begin to flow through your life.

Dear God,
Help me to keep open to Your love,
that I may feel You in all places
and hear Your voice in all things.

PEACE
PRINCIPLES

8

Living on purpose

Examine your heart
Live from what you know to be true.

Your yearnings and visions of the Boundless must become grounded in the practical minutiae of daily life or your spirituality is simply entertainment.

To live on purpose you must first clarify your purpose. Clear intentions ensure your spirituality leads you deeper into truth not traps. Without clear and loving intentions, no amount of meditation, prayer and inspiration will transform your being. Without direct contact with the Boundless, a moral life will not blossom into an inspired one. Both the mystic vertical and the practical horizontal dimensions are necessary to realise your Divinity and live as the presence of Boundless Love that you truly are.

In my initial years on the path I was pathologically impatient. In a rush to cut my teeth into what I considered more important mystical practices I initially skipped past exploring ethics. Focusing too much on the vertical, I came unstuck because my foundations were not solid enough. When I began to embrace ethics as peace principles that supported my inner freedom, my awareness and my relationships began to flower. I learnt that ethics free up your energy and help birth your highest aspirations. While not the most glamorous aspect of spirituality, having clear ethical principles accelerates your awakening process and cuts through any extraneous psychic clutter.

There is no conflict between religions on the importance of ethics. The Buddhist code, the yogic precepts, the Jewish, Christian and Islamic commandments and the values at the heart of most native religions, all share virtually identical ideas. All speak of the importance of truthfulness, non-harming, respecting others and kindness. Ethics are the ancient, time-tested midwives of the soul.

Traditionally, in many monasteries, ashrams and esoteric schools, consciousness-raising practices were not taught until a pupil could demonstrate a clear understanding of their ethical principles. This is not simply a clever ploy to weed out the spiritual riffraff. Grounding yourself in ethics before giving you esoteric practice helps to ensure that your spirituality leads to freedom not delusion.

Life cannot be compartmentalised

I find it hard to feel at one with the Boundless Love of my essence if I have spent my day skirting the issue, jumping ahead of the supermarket queue, acting selfishly or simply neglecting to be kind. Doing things that make me feel bad about myself makes soul contact harder.

Everything comes to sit with you in meditation. The level of kindness you offer to family, friends and work colleagues; the openness of your communication, your degree of self-honesty and how you handle your finances, all impact on your awareness. To God, there are no compartments. Being unclear or unloving in one area will hold you back in others. Returning into integrity in any one aspect brings more freedom to the rest. Every part of life is spiritual and thus deserving of your loving attention.

Ethics are not guilt-inducing rules you must obey to 'become a better person', but guidelines to embrace because they make your life simpler and happier. Ethics are meant to be a kind and practical help to you for living on purpose. Whenever you fall out of alignment with your own integrity, this is what it can cost you.

You lose yourself

Untruthful, unkind and unloving thoughts and actions produce painful emotions such as fear, guilt and anger. This rocks you off your centre and causes unhappiness. To hurt another is to hurt yourself.

You lose peace of mind

Destructive mental and behavioural patterns can arise, such as the desire for revenge, obsessions, addictions, paranoia and other fearful states. For example, lying causes you to be frightened of being found out, which can produce defensiveness, guilt and aggression. Being unkind makes you suspect that others are hostile and antagonistic towards you. Unethical living causes your defence systems to go on red alert, driving your wounds further underground.

Your relationships suffer

Your un-mindful states of being have toxic effects on others. The places where you are not integrated can sabotage intimacy, communication and joy in your relationships.

You preach but don't really practise

It is a common trap to tell others about your spiritual beliefs while forgetting to love, accept, respect and see the perfection in the person before you. This causes you to feel separate.

Life becomes stressful and unnecessarily complicated

This leaves you feeling guilty, scattered and far from whole.

Your spiritual progress is impaired

Without clear intentions, a spiritual path can become a defence against old wounds rather than a vehicle to help heal them. Unethical living drains your spiritual resources and pulls you off course.

Take a spiritual inventory

Take stock of how on purpose you are spiritually by taking half an hour with a notebook to go through the following exercise.

⌒ Set your intention to look at your life honestly and with kindness. Close your eyes, take some breaths and relax into the present moment. Ask the presence of God's Boundless Love, an angel, helper or guide to be with you in this exercise.

⌒ Reflect upon the core of your spiritual path or belief. What is it exactly?
Try to write it down in one sentence. For example:
  'Opening to Boundless Love.'
  'Living from my essence.'
  'Awakening into enlightenment.'

⌒ Reflect on the essence of what your path asks you to do. Write this down
in a maximum of four points. For example, practising:
  Kindness.
  Honesty.
  Mindfulness.
  Compassion.

⌒ To what percentage are you actually doing these things in the following
areas of your life?
  With your family?
  With your partner/spouse?
  With your children?
  With your friends?
  With your job and work colleagues?
  With money and practical arrangements?
  With your body and physical needs?
  With your community?

⌒ What supports you in living spiritually on purpose?

⌒ What hampers you?

Assessing yourself compassionately

Underneath every area you are not living on purpose or acting
unethically lie hidden feelings of guilt. When I created this
spiritual inventory and went through the questions myself, I
identified my spiritual path as, 'Healing the blocks to Boundless
Love.' This asks me to practise honesty, forgiveness, loving kindness and surrender. In the area of intimate relationships, family,
work and community I was doing well. However, I was shocked to
see that in my relationship to my body I was often judgemental,
controlling and unkind; quite the opposite of my spiritual intentions.

Exploring more deeply, I saw that this was the area where I had been judging myself and playing out hidden feelings of guilt. No wonder my body had been feeling tired, achy, sleep deprived and less than vital. Recognising this was a wonderful wake-up call that put me on the road to practising my spirituality more mindfully in this area. It led me into greater peace and health.

Embrace whatever arises from your spiritual inventory. Be accountable for your actions without condemning yourself for being human. Few people consciously intend to cause harm, yet in a sometimes harsh and challenging world it can be easy to stray from the path. Everyone has areas where they are tempted to cut corners, omit to be kind or bend the truth. Your short-comings are the places where you are unconscious, ignorant or wounded.

Be willing to face these areas and open yourself to heal their causes with compassion not condemnation. Punishing self-talk will not inspire you to healing. The truth should set you free, not beat you up.

Open to greater innocence

Too often I notice people becoming despondent when they realise their mistakes. Discovering what trips you up is cause for celebration not despair. Your honesty places you at the threshold of a new level of freedom. You cannot change that which you cannot see. While you are unaware of mistakes, they run you. However, once identified, the process of release can begin.

The areas that your spiritual inventory highlighted are the zones in your life where guilt and judgement has been camping out. Facing exactly what drives you away from your centre offers you a doorway to feeling innocent again. You have never been, and will never be, Divinely condemned. A mistake calls for loving correction not punishment. Be willing to know that whatever mistakes you have made, your innocence is not lost to you.

Many spiritually committed people forget that they can ask for Divine help with any problem they confront. Taking your short-comings to prayer for release is the simplest, quickest and most effective way to move forward with anything. Raise whatever areas where you are not living on purpose to prayer for healing.

Here's how:

* Thank God for helping you see where you hold yourself back.
* Pray for a deeper understanding of exactly what drives you to sabotage yourself in this way.
* Pray for help in forgiving yourself.
* Give to God your willingness to live on purpose.
* Ask for help in feeling innocent and whole again.

Inviting the Boundless to help you live more ethically supports you in feeling innocent, free, happy and whole. It is the most certain method of quickening your personal spiritual awakening.

Ground in kindness, truth and love

Lining up the ethical codes from spiritual traditions east and west, the three perennial themes that dominate are kindness, truth and love.

Kindness is a force of conscious harmlessness that renders you powerfully happy. Kindness encompasses the universal directive of not killing or harming from the most obvious to the more subtle aspects of not harming another's feelings or killing off their joy. Beyond simply not causing harm, to be kind is to cultivate an active intention to nurture the wellbeing of self and others. Kindness works to alleviate whatever suffering it encounters with gentle humanity, building the spirits of all it touches.

Truth brings safety and clarity as well as freedom to all. Commitment to self-honesty is the primary foundation for all spiritual enquiry, and honesty the basis for healthy relationships, families and communities. The degree of truth dictates the degree of trust. Truth is the foundation of all ethical codes, encompassing non-stealing, non-lying and basic decency, but truth is not brutal. In the Buddhist eight-fold path, right speech is defined as truthful, appropriately timed and kind to the ear. If your intention is to be genuinely kind, the truth can be spoken and heard without attack.

When you are identified with love and grounded in love, kindness and honesty come naturally. To love is to actively reach from your heart to the heart of another to give warmth, care, companionship, support and affection. Your love removes the harsh barriers of defensiveness born of fear. Your love blesses everyone. Underneath all appearances, giving and receiving love is the true need in any situation, and the primary purpose for which you are here on earth. True love is universal, not simply personal. To love wholly is to attain Divinity.

Set a conscious daily intention to be kind, truthful and loving and you will experience deep peace of mind. You will be a peaceful presence to others. You will discover more of who you really are and why you are here. Let your thoughts, your actions, indeed your whole life be grounded in these three principles and you cannot stray far.

If ever in doubt as to whether you are spiritually on purpose or not, ask:

* Is it kind?
* Is it truthful?
* Is it loving?

'One with God, I am united with my purpose.
My life must succeed in every way.'

Alan Cohen

The ten invitations

For today, do that which disturbs no one.
Embrace that which brings peace.
Let life become beautiful.

Every spiritual path offers practical guidelines to help navigate you through life's obstacles into greater peace and freedom: the Buddhist eight-fold path, the Judeo Christian Ten Command-ments, and the yogic Niyanas. Historically, these guidelines have often been presented as dogmatic lists of rules to be obeyed out of fear. Often warped by political agendas, this has turned many away from the profound states of being that the heart of the teachings offer.

The God of Boundless Love that I know sends invitations, never commandments. You are given complete free will to respond or reject the invitation. Love does not need to bully you into action. Love does not demand nor insist, even if the path you choose leads to untold pain. Love simply offers freely and waits on your welcome.

Seek universal truths behind dogmas

Mystics know that within any ancient teaching lie powerful universal keys to peace. An excellent example is the Ten Commandments. Even if you did not have a religious upbringing you will have been raised with their principles as they form the basis of the western legal system. Have you ever thought to reflect upon them as a source of spiritual inspiration? Have you ever questioned their true meaning and relevance to your life today?

If you choose to see them as loving invitations rather than fearful commandments, they act as guiding angels, ushering you towards the fulfilment of your soul's yearning. Each invitation contains keys to make your life work better, encouraging inner harmony, loving relationships, good financial, emotional and sexual health, and peace in your family, community and world.

Smile at the rebel in you that may resist that which in the past has been presented as rules to obey to appease a demanding, punitive God. Welcome these as wonderful peace principles; supportive structures to help apply your highest intentions. Any one of them, understood deeply and embraced fully, has the power to turn your life around. It is in this light that I offer you my reflections of the Ten Commandments, taken from the books of *Exodus* and *Deuteronomy*.

The Universal Invitations

1 'I am the Lord your God. You shall have no other gods before Me.'

The invitation: *To make your spirituality the central pillar that supports the rest of your life.*

It is easy to make obtaining a bigger house, a swankier car, a more prestigious job and more money your god. Your god is that which you make most important, your homing beacon. What's yours? Although material goals and possessions are not inherently bad, they become traps when you make them more important than the inner gold.

My friend and mentor Tom Carpenter continually inspires me to make my spirituality more central. Whether sharing insights to a group or buying bread at the supermarket, Tom keeps his spiritual alignment, listening from within for truth to guide his every word and action. The impact this has on others is nothing short of extraordinary. Tom radiates an exceptional level of love and clarity. Watching him go about his day is a teaching in itself.

Make your spirituality the cornerstone of your life because it feeds your every faculty. With a strong spiritual foundation, rain and storms, stresses and challenges can come and you will be better able to meet them with peace and wisdom. Your motivation becomes purer, your actions driven more by what is good for all, not just towards fulfilling your own ego wants and desires. Ironically, you will find every other aspect of your life becomes more successful.

2 'You shall not bow down and worship any idols.'

The invitation: *To let go of unhealthy attachments and nurture the deeper calling of your higher aspirations.*

What are you unhealthily attached to? What keeps you in bondage? What do you idolise? Your answers reveal where you delay peace and happiness, hampering your spiritual progress by getting lost in illusions.

An idol is a substitute for the real thing. Perhaps your soul sabotage takes the form of unhelpful addictions to food, alcohol or harmful substances. Perhaps you have become addicted to negative self-perceptions and ways of relating. Perhaps money, power and status have become more important to you than love. Break free from unhelpful habits by releasing the fears and false beliefs that drive them.

Anyone who has broken free of addictive patterns via the methods taught within 12-step programmes knows this as a spiritual journey in itself. It requires self-honesty, courage, willingness, support and a strong spiritual foundation. Millions of people have proved that even the most deeply ingrained negative addictions and patterns can be healed. So can yours.

3 'You shall not take the name of the Lord your God in vain.'

The invitation: *To heal the causes of anger and insecurity that may lead you to shoot out poisonous arrows through your words.*

Examine closely what causes you to move into destructive emotional states that cause yourself and others pain. Be aware that no emotion is inherently bad if you simply listen to it with acceptance. Paying attention to your own feelings (not blaming another for them and insisting they need to change in order for you to feel better) helps you see a truer way forward.

My friend Amanda is a person of tremendous dignity who once had a big problem with anger. Deeply compassionate by nature, she worked as a counsellor in addition to raising four children alone. A pillar of strength to many, Amanda frequently overlooked her own needs. Whenever she was criticised or unappreciated Amanda would slip into resentment and blow her top. She would swear and say harsh and unkind words, which afterwards left her feeling guilty. This caused painful repercussions in her relationships with those she most loved.

For years Amanda tried to control her anger, but however hard she tried it didn't work. Later she began to tackle what caused her to 'shoot off at the mouth'. Amanda faced false beliefs about being 'not good enough', old wounds from childhood around being criticised, and feeling overly responsible for others. Amanda's insecurity led her into to a pattern of self-sacrifice, which caused her to feel angry. Beginning to forgive herself, forgive others from the past, listen more compassionately to her own needs and ask others for help, the rampaging woman inside calmed down. Then the outbursts ceased of themselves.

4 'Remember the Sabbath day and keep it holy.'

The invitation: *To carve out regular space to unhook from daily pressures and connect with what's truly meaningful.*

Taking a Sabbath is more important now than it ever was. The advent of new technologies designed to make modern life easier have simply increased expectations of how much can be done with the minimum outlay in the shortest possible time. Modern Western life has become unbalanced and fraught with stress.

My friend Elaine takes one day a week to spend in simplicity and silence. Every Wednesday she nurtures her soul by pottering about the house, cooking, meditating, reading, being still – all in silence. Elaine has trained her family, friends and clients not to expect her to engage verbally with them on this day, which they honour. It acts as a regular retreat that gives her untold spiritual strength to take into the next week.

What would your Sabbath look like? Begin carving out a regular time for soul nourishment, beginning with a few hours a week to a full day. Use this time to slow down, unhook from anything work-related, meditate, pray, read inspirational books and spend time relaxing with family and loved ones. Spaciousness breeds inspiration.

5 'Honour your father and mother.'

The invitation: *To respect your parents for giving you life, and commit yourself to healing whatever difficulties exist in your relationship.*

Holding on to grievances with your parents has a destructive effect on your whole life, and will cause you to sabotage your relationships, your happiness and your peace of mind.

That which you blame your parents for doing to you, you are probably already doing to yourself, or to someone else. Let go of blame. You release yourself as you forgive your parents. Where there is difficulty between you, know that there is no problem beyond a miracle. Your sincere willingness for release will guide you towards its actuality.

Andrew, an advertising executive in his thirties, left England to carve out a new life for himself in New York. One day he admitted to me that the real reason for his move was to escape his mother's constant criticism. In her eyes, Andrew could do no right. It had become too painful to bear. During our sessions, Andrew realised that his mother's criticism was in truth mirroring the relentless criticism Andrew dished out to himself in his own mind. Andrew had inherited a pattern of self-criticism from his mother, who criticised herself as harshly as she did Andrew.

Andrew worked with some loving kindness meditations to bring compassion to both himself and his mother. In his inner vision, Andrew learned to give his mother the love her harsh criticism was calling out for. The relationship immediately began to improve. Giving to his mother what he wanted to receive began to transform the relationship beyond all recognition, and freed Andrew to be more authentic and at peace.

6 'You shall not murder.'

The invitation: *To cease attacking physically, mentally, emotionally, spiritually.*

Few people intend to physically kill or attack another, yet it is easy to overlook the mental and emotional violence of harsh judgements. Any arrows you direct outwards on any level have painful impacts on the person you direct them to and a destructive impact on your peace of mind.

There was a period in my late twenties when I experienced painful amounts of projection, jealousy and sniping from others. Being back-stabbed felt hurtful and unfair. Feeling very vulnerable, I asked the question in meditation one morning, 'How can I feel safer?' I received an answer loud and clear, 'Stop attacking.' Then I was shown how every harsh thought I had about anyone is a form of attack that would inevitably backfire on me. My inner guidance coached me to soften my judgements, or at the very least not take them so seriously. Interestingly, attacks began to come my way with less frequency and force, and I learnt to be less affected by others' fearful projections.

Even if you don't agree with another's actions, be willing to let kindness take the place of criticism, condemnation and judgement. You will become one less violent force on the planet.

7 'You shall not commit adultery.'

The invitation: *To be true and faithful to your promises – physically, emotionally, mentally and sexually.*

Adultery is a form of betrayal, which encompasses yet transcends your sexual behaviour. Aim first not to betray yourself by being faithful to your own sense of integrity and listening to your inner knowing. Then you are less likely to make half-hearted commitments out of obligation, that you inevitably break.

Be faithful to other people by only making promises you are able and willing to fulfil joyfully. Find the courage to say, 'Yes' when you mean it, and 'No' when you know you cannot give yourself whole-heartedly. Conscious commitment frees, not binds. Be careful, though, that you do not shy from commitment, as this simply places a ceiling on intimacy and trust. Just be clear what you commit to, and then intend to be faithful to it.

When you are true and faithful to yourself, and to the promises you give to others, everyone thrives. Innocence returns, relationships deepen, creativity reaches new heights and sex becomes a sacred bridge to higher love.

8 'You shall not steal.'

The invitation: *To heal the belief in lack that may cause you to rob another to get your perceived needs met.*

Behind the universal directive not to steal or take what is not freely given, is a teaching of abundance. Stealing or trampling on others to get what you want assumes there isn't enough to go around. Although you may struggle financially, spiritually every grace is given you. The key is to become more open to receiving it.

Robert and I lived for seven years with two highly entertaining cats called Great and Wonderful. At feeding time they would meow, scrap with one another and create such frenzy that it would require one of us to hold down the cats, and the other to distribute their food into bowls. One evening Robert was away and I was trying to feed the cats on my own. They were going through their usual routine, and it became impossible to put the bowls of food they were screeching for down on the floor for them to eat. In frustration I shouted at them, 'Will you please shut up and get out of the way so I can give you what you're asking for.' A split second later I laughed out loud at the recognition that God probably feels the same way with me.

When you learn to become a better receiver it is natural to respect other people and their property. Opening to receive the grace that's always being offered to you makes it easier to accomplish your goals without stripping someone else bare in the process. To know that there is no lack is to be deeply at peace.

9 'You shall not bear false witness against your neighbour.'

The invitation: *To witness and support the highest truth in others.*

My friend Romy is one of the most impressive people I know for one simple reason: she never says an unkind word about anyone. In the company of others who may be gossiping, she never joins in, only says a few quiet words about their virtues. Romy is no Pollyanna, but a highly creative, successful businesswoman. Clearly her commitment to support others and not tear them down feeds her personal vibrancy. Gossip is never harmless, and diminishes everyone associated with it. My husband Robert calls gossip 'social farting': smelly hot air that makes life unnecessarily unpleasant.

Aim to bear true witness. Seek out the highest truth in others. To see anyone truly is to see God. The single most powerful thing you can do to help anyone live their best self is to hold the vision of them as inherently whole and acceptable. Bearing true witness is also the most immediate way to know your own wholeness and innocence, because everything you give, you receive. Experiment with bearing true witness towards everyone you see, think of or speak to today, and your own Divinity will become much clearer to you.

10 'You shall not covet your neighbour's possessions.'

The invitation: *To transform envy through taking joy in the good fortune of others, learning to appreciate what you have.*

When you see people who appear to 'have it all' – success, love, beauty, brains, talent, money – do you think, 'How wonderful! Good for them', or do you snipe, 'Lucky bitch!' As long as you are jealous of others for having what you want, you will block yourself from receiving the fulfilment of your own dreams.

'Sympathetic joy' is an important Buddhist cornerstone. It means to take joy in the joy and good fortune of others, wishing for them what you want for yourself. My Buddhist friend Kathy is one of the happiest people I know. Although her life has not always been a magic carpet ride, Kathy actively celebrates others' blessings, and is masterful at enjoying what she has. Everyone notices how exceptionally joyous and radiant she is.

Sympathetic joy is an unconscious affirmation of abundance. It helps you recognise blessings, and it draws further blessings towards you. Transform jealousy into inspiration. Follow others' examples and step forward more fully into your own giftedness. Let every person you see who has what you want become a living affirmation that you too can have a wonderful life.

When you decline the invitation ...

As you grow in awareness you will realise that each moment is an invitation to be more present, true, open, loving and wise. This is the universal curriculum. Be absolutely clear on this: you will never be spiritually condemned for making a mistake. Any invitation you do not rise to will simply be presented again in the future. The Divine attitude to your mistakes is simply to 'try again'. There is no sin. You can never miss your 'chance'.

Although you can delay your awakening with resistance, denial and ignorance, your awakening into Boundless Love is inevitable. Just as a magnet below a sheet of paper draws the iron shavings to itself, so your soul is inexplicably drawn by the magnetism of God and your true Self. Free will does not necessarily mean you can choose the journey, simply that you can elect how long and difficult you wish it to be. Choosing to resist universal invitations just makes life more painful than necessary. Instead, let these ten universal invitations become your peace principles.

Each time you rise to accept an invitation
you grow in power and in peace.

10

Practical spirituality

If the kingdom of heaven is within,
Are you visiting regularly?

Regular spiritual practice is the means to open you to a sustained experience of Boundless Love.

Learning to live in a state of peace, love and truth takes more than thinking pink fluffy thoughts: it takes discipline, patience and courage. Spiritual practice is a radical commitment to a different way of being, an inner response to life that begins to reverse your conditioning and loosen your identification with separation and fear. It helps you live your highest intentions and crafts you into the person you want to be. Discovering a method of spiritual practice that works for you is like acquiring golden tools through which to excavate your true brilliance. There is nothing you yearn for that spiritual practice cannot give. However, there are no short cuts.

When I began to carve out daily time for conscious contact with God, the spiritual principles I had been exploring began to grow roots and bear fruit in my daily life. Grace shifted from an idea I understood intellectually to a practical force for transformation. New insights came flooding in, and my growth and healing gathered real momentum.

Today I receive so much from my daily practice that I do not know how anyone gets by without one. The more wholeheartedly and consistently you come to God, the greater the benefits you will reap. Spiritual practice feeds your higher faculties and strengthens your capacity to receive guidance. Thus it becomes an extremely potent addition to your everyday problem-solving repertoire.

Just as it is unreasonable to expect to be in peak physical

condition if you do not eat healthily, get enough rest and take regular physical exercise, so you cannot expect spiritual principles to flower into a life of greater freedom, wisdom and joy without regular periods of conscious contact with God. Spiritual practice strengthens your inner spiritual muscles, and allows the principle of love to root itself back into your mind. You develop the capacity to apply higher wisdom where it counts. Old fears, past wounds and daily stress have a place to unwind, and more of your Boundless Self comes to the fore.

Make time for soul nourishment

The Catholic mystic St Francis de Sales once said that, 'Half an hour's meditation each day is essential – except when you are very busy. Then a full hour is needed.' I have found that increasing my commitment to spiritual practice when under stress helps me tap into greater levels of grace, strength and wisdom, which better enables me to rise to challenges rather than become swamped by them.

Easton is an old friend whom Robert and I had not seen much of since we left Birmingham. One of those people who really lights up a room with his clarity and warmth, it was a joy to see Easton on our doorstep. A highly skilled counsellor, Easton looked positively aglow, and I anticipated hearing wonderful news of his life. Easton told us that in the space of four years his wife Debra had spiralled down from a vibrant, energetic woman in her early forties to a life devoid of most of her faculties. Rapidly degenerating with motor neuron disease, the medical team had withheld official diagnosis for fear of being sued for emotional distress should they be wrong. By the time the diagnosis was given, Debra was beyond effective treatment.

Now completely dependent and not even able to speak or turn herself over in bed, Easton and their two teenage children are the only people who can understand Debra's communication signals. This means that Easton had become his wife's full-time carer in addition to fathering his children, managing the household and working to keep afloat financially. On a good night, he gets a maximum of four hours' sleep. Stunned to hear this, I asked Easton, 'How are you coping?' He answered without hesitation, 'Meditation practice.' Easton told me that he gets up at 4 am just so he can fit a full two hours meditation into his day. 'I know that the strength, equanimity and energy with which to hold the kind of attitude to this that I want to hold comes directly from my time with the Creator', he said.

Furthermore, Easton went on to tell me that his wife Debra insists on being woken to join him in meditation, even though she is in intense pain. Debra's attitude to her situation is so extraordinarily positive Easton feels inspired to match it. Hearing him speak of Debra succeeding in making her entire family laugh themselves silly every day, even though unable to speak, move or do anything for herself, moved me to tears. I thought to myself, 'If they can find the time to meditate, anyone can.'

Meditation brings out your best

I can instantly spot a person who has an active spiritual practice. They glow with inner peace. Their capacity for joy and compassion is broad. Much less emotionally reactive, those who take time out for spiritual nourishment have a quiet wisdom and equanimity about them. They live happier, more focused, less agitated lives. Under pressure, they are better able to keep a perspective. Evolving a daily spiritual practice and making it the central hub of your life's wheel is singularly the greatest favour you could give yourself. Rumi gives a superb analogy: 'What nine months does for an embryo, 40 early mornings with God will do for your growing awareness.'

Your ego will throw up all kinds of good excuses why giving yourself at least half an hour a day for spiritual practice is impossible. I have heard them all. I also know single mothers who get up an hour earlier to have a time of soul nourishment, busy professionals who get to work early while it is quiet to clear their minds before the day begins. When you register how much spiritual practice can give you, you will make it as much of a priority as brushing your teeth.

Commit but don't enslave yourself

Commit to spiritual practice not to reach some spiritual summit, but to awaken consciously to the reality that Boundless Love is always with you. Commit to regular time with God because it feeds and sustains your highest vision, but do not make it an obligation. The last thing you need is to project guilt onto spiritual practice, adding it to your 'must do' list, and beating up on yourself if you fail.

Joey is a bright and inspired artist in her mid-thirties. She had been around many approaches to spirituality for years. Having found what felt like her true path, Joey was feeling bad for failing to commit to the space for silence she needed. When she eventually sat to meditate Joey found no peace, only huge resistance. Making an intelligent choice not to struggle with this, Joey asked inwardly, 'What is it that I really need?' The answer came, 'Stillness.' Joey set her intention to stop at various intervals within her day and open to stillness. This brought her out of resistance, and before long Joey was looking forward to her morning spiritual practice sessions.

The quality of your practice is not governed so much by the length of time you spend within, but the quality of intention you bring to it. Commit to conscious Divine contact daily knowing that the effort you create will feed and sustain you in ways you can only imagine. If you are already committed to spiritual practice, wonderful. Consider adding new dimensions to it. You are constantly evolving, thus your spiritual practice needs to evolve also.

Here are some practical pointers that will help to establish spiritual practice as a habit or deepen your existing practice.

Set aside a particular time

Unless you allocate specific time to go within, you will never get around to it. First thing in the morning is the ideal time for meditation, taking a shorter period for reflection, prayer and releasing mental stress in the early evening. Going within as soon as possible after you have woken up, bathed and dressed helps you embark on the day spiritually prepared. This strengthens your capacity to remember love's vision and apply it throughout the day.

If you have children you will need to be more organised. Perhaps go to bed a little earlier in the evenings so as to have the energy to rise earlier than your child. If this is impossible, keep a helpful spiritual reminder or prayer by your bed to set your intention first thing, and then carve out time to sit silently after they have gone to school or day care. I know women with young babies who organise a helper or friend to come in for an hour in the mornings just so they can meditate. Where there is a will there is a way. If you are a night owl perhaps evenings would be a better time, only when you are tired it is too easy to have a glass of wine and watch television. Assess your lifestyle honestly to find what time of day would be most conducive for you to go within, and commit to it. Ask for the support you need. Know that nourishing yourself spiritually will mean that others get a calmer, clearer, stronger, more loving person to live with.

Create a sacred space

Psychologically, it helps inspire a desire to go within if you have created a peaceful, beautiful environment. Robert and I have a meditation room in our home, which is used only for meditation, reflection and counselling. This is our sacred space, containing visual reminders of what is most meaningful to us. It has become the soul of our home, a powerful metaphor reminding us in busy times that there is always a space we can enter that is calm. Whatever havoc may have accumulated in the rest of the house, we do not allow our meditation room to get dusty or cluttered.

You do not have to create a whole room, but choosing a chair or space where you will go within assists your unconscious mind to register your commitment. It need not be grand, just clean, calming and private. Always sit comfortably rather than lie down, ensuring you have the support needed to maintain a good posture. In that way your body will not distract from the quieting process.

Within this space you may want to create an altar, containing symbols of that which evoke for you the sacred. This may be a picture of a saint or teacher, an inspirational book, artwork or objects from nature. For me, I like to have something living, such as a flower or plant to remind me that my spirit is alive and blossoming, and a candle to light as a beginning ritual. This is highly personal, so create the space in the most meaningful way to you and then dedicate it as your zone.

Walk with mighty companions

Although no one can go within for you, opening to receive support and encouragement from others will take you much further into the Boundless than you can go yourself. If you have left the support structures within conventional religion behind, you will need to generate new ones. If you cannot find even a single person who also wants to open to a sustained experience of the Boundless, pray to gravitate towards one.

When you choose to receive support, a buddy or even a group of them will appear. Wherever I go in the world, I always manage to find Divine companions. Just as the might of heaven walks with you spiritually, you need not walk alone on an earthly level. If you absolutely cannot find anyone, you may want to seek the help of a spiritual counsellor or guide (listed in the back of this book), who will have been trained to listen, support and help facilitate your spiritual growth.

Do you need a teacher?

In essence, everyone is your teacher. Indeed, life is your teacher. If you pay attention and regard everyone as either sending you Divine feedback or mirroring your own ego, you will recognise that you are being led by an inner teacher who is guiding you at all times. The methods for opening to receive guidance I described in the chapter on Inner Wisdom will strengthen your capacity to listen to your inner teacher.

Sometimes you will be led to an external teacher who will be best able to illuminate the way forward at a particular juncture of your development. The deeper into the Boundless you go, the more subtle the traps can become, and a good teacher can help navigate your way through. Do not seek a guru, but if you come across a genuine teacher or guide be very thankful. You can always recognise them through their profound love and compassion for all humanity. They will embody their message and want nothing more than for you to know the truth of your being. A genuine teacher will empower you with tools, instruction and practical methods with which to free your spirit, and will continually point you back to the truth within your own heart, not ask for blind obedience. Let your inner teacher guide you where and to whom.

Create daily reminders

Once you commit to regular spiritual practice you will begin to realise how attached to fearful egocentric thinking you are. Do not despair. Accept where you are and create anchors throughout your day to remind you of the truth at the centre of your being. Short prayers or favourite quotes from an inspirational text help you to keep centred amidst activity, and help you re-centre when you fall into stressful states.

Create such reminders at your desk, in your car, by your bedside and in your wallet. The world we live in can be very hypnotic. Do not berate yourself for wandering into fear, instead find creative ways to anchor yourself in higher awareness. I once took to writing the guidance I received in meditation each morning on the palm of my hand. Just noticing throughout the day that there was ink on my hand jogged my memory of the guidance and the experience of love that accompanied it. See every activity as an opportunity to be present and open to the truth.

Just do it!

Although there will be days when unexpected things happen to intercept your quiet time, if you are committed this will be the occasion not the rule. Pray for help: 'Dear God, help inspire me to want to go within', or, 'Help me value myself enough to nourish my soul', or, 'Lend me courage to retrieve the wonderful gifts you have placed within me.'

You will have good days and bad days, times when you experience deep peace and wisdom, and other days of spiritual static. This is normal. Do not compare yourself with others' experience (people often exaggerate their spiritual experiences anyway). Just keep showing up regularly in your sacred space. It is not about 'making progress', but coming more deeply into the present moment, where you will gradually awake to the luminous beauty of who you are and what truly is.

Find your spiritual practice

There are a thousand routes to the Boundless Love of God and your true Self. Find a practice that you enjoy and that feeds your deepest need. I hear far too much sectarian talk of 'this is the best path or practice'. Any reasonable practice will work if your intention is sincere. Focus on finding what is right for you.

Over the coming chapters I guide you through the practices that have made the most difference to me, and have had the greatest impact on the many people I have shared them with. Some are adapted from ancient traditions, others have come to me through inner guidance. I have sectioned them into:

* **The vast heart**: Practises to open the heart, accessing boundless levels of love and compassion.
* **Divine mind**: Practises to cultivate calm, wisdom and higher thinking.
* **Healing the blocks to love**: Transformational practices to heal old wounds
* **Spiritual resistance**: Guidance to help navigate you through the subtle traps that can trip you up as you walk back into Boundless Love.
* **No boundaries**: To help integrate expanded states of being into relationships, supporting you to fulfil your spiritual purpose.

Many meditation teachers believe that you should find one method of spiritual practice and stick to it for life. Personally, I am wary of making the form of spiritual practice more important than its essence. Your practice will evolve as you evolve. A good method is one that transforms your weaknesses and enhances your natural strengths. Your spiritual practice should be as multi-dimensional as you are. In each of us there is a lover, an intellectual, a mystic and a servant. Each of these dimensions feeds one another. A rounded spiritual life should nurture and stretch every part.

I suggest you sit with each practice for three days at a time, or more if you like. There is no rush to get through them – each practice is independently worth its weight in gold. When you have gone through them all, craft a daily practice out of whatever practices fed you the most, and the ones you had the strongest aversion to. It is often the methods you initially greet with the strongest resistance that have the most transforming effects.

Remember that meditation and prayer are not spiritual gymnastics, just simple and natural ways to make your soul fly. The more wholly you give yourself to the practices, the more receptive you will be to their transforming effects. Enjoy!

Why just look at the sumptuous banquet
When we are all hungry for grace? Let's eat.

Part IV

THE VAST
HEART

Begin with gratitude

'You can tell how evolved someone is from how grateful they are for all the gifts of God.'

Sri Ramakrishna

Gratitude offers an inner sanctuary of joy and abundance in a world full of cynicism, defensiveness and fear. It is the simplest means to open up the vast power of your heart. Gratitude interrupts negative emotional states, melts destructive victim mindsets, and releases you back to profound peace.

Gratitude amplifies your capacity to receive. The Divine does not particularly need your thanks, but you need to recognise the gifts you have been given that you may receive them fully. In receiving fully, you have so much more to give. Gratitude is a choice to focus on what you have, rather than to indulge the illusion of lack by complaining. Gratitude catapults your soul into higher states of being.

On our most recent trip to India, Robert and I visited Bodhgaya, where Buddha attained enlightenment underneath the Bodhi tree. This significant pilgrimage site is rich in monks, beautiful temples and peaceful ambience, yet materially it is one of the very poorest regions in India. Hunger, hardship and homelessness are commonplace. On our arrival, three teenage boys befriended us, insisting on becoming our unofficial guides. Hearing that we wanted to find a quiet place to meditate, they took us on a journey beyond the main town to a simple outdoor temple amidst rice fields and rivers. There we meditated, witnessed by 15 or so beggars praying for us to come out of meditation soon to give them some rupees!

Next to this temple was a six by twelve feet hut being used as a school. Eager for the children to have a chance to practice their English, the teacher invited us inside. We had fun engaging a few words and many gestures with the 30 children, aged from four to eight. They came from desperately poor villages where most of them slept with their families underneath roofs made of nothing more than a few poles and old pieces of plastic. Directed by their teacher, the children stood and sang to us the only song they knew in English. The words to this song were:

'Dear God, thank you for my mother, father, sister, brother,
the sky, the sun, the rain the fields, this school …
I love you God, I love you God.
Thank you Thank you.'

In their dire poverty, without even the resources to buy pencils and paper to learn how to read and write, 30 children were whole-heartedly thanking their Creator for everything they had.

I was moved to tears witnessing them singing. I wished that everyone I knew who had ever complained of life being problematic and joyless could see the beauty of such exuberant gratitude and devotion. These children, with precarious futures ahead of them, and materially nothing to their name, possessed an abundant wealth of happiness and spirituality that no external hardship could extinguish. Their teacher later informed us that the spirit of gratitude and the words 'thank you' is the first lesson they learn.

Whatever you focus on expands

Cultivating a thankful heart is the fertile soil in which the other virtues of kindness, love, forgiveness, patience and trust grow. Yet how easy it is to focus on what's gone 'wrong', the one person who was rude or unkind to you, the one apparent setback that unfolded contrary to your plans. Choosing to focus on life's negatives can grossly cloud your perception of life, until negatives are all you see. Choose instead to focus on the few small things that are right in your world, and your life will immediately become enriched with hope.

No matter how difficult a time you are having, there are always blessings peeping through the cracks of your life if you are open to receive them: a smile from a stranger, the kindness of a friend, the tenderness of loved ones, an able body and mind, enough food to eat, the ability to read and enrich yourself. These simple gifts are the Boundless loving you through avenues you can more readily accept.

If you examine your life closely, you will see causes to be grateful for something. Explore more deeply and you will realise that life is profoundly graced with many simple but extraordinary miracles that you have been overlooking. Contemplating your blessings in the midst of great challenges begins to open your heart to receive them. This brings the awareness that you are blessed and profoundly loved. Receiving the awareness of how blessed and loved you are, how could you not feel happy? What then could block you giving the gift of your love?

The practice of gratitude plays a central part in every path. For instance, in the Jewish tradition every prayer begins with giving thanks for what is: 'Blessed art Thou, O Lord our God, King of the Universe, who blesses and sanctifies (the food we are about to eat, the water in which we will bathe, the wine which we will drink, etc.)'. The Hebrew prayer book offers prayers of thanksgiving for the most seemingly ordinary activities, including prayers for eating, prayers for love-making, even prayers for going to the lavatory. My Jewish friends who practise this level of thanksgiving emit vibrant joy and reverence for life, even though they have all known sufferings harsher than most.

Gratitude is magnetic in that it attracts to you greater blessings. The more grateful you are, the more you will have to be grateful about. No matter what your life circumstance, gratitude is a potent multi-vitamin for your soul.

Begin the practice of gratitude

Each moment is a good time to offer thanks for what you have. However, your mind is usually most relaxed and therefore most fertile in the first and last waking hours of each day. Where you direct your energy first thing in the morning sets the rudder of your awareness for the day. The consciousness you go to sleep on impacts how you wake up the next morning. Use these two pivotal times to practise gratitude, and every other spiritual practice and principle meaningful to you will come alive.

Night-time gratitude

As you are lying in bed at night, give thanks to the Boundless for ten gifts that exist in your life, or that have occurred that day. You will probably need to search hard to begin with. Begin by thanking God for the things you normally take for granted, like the ability to breathe, the ability to think, having food to eat, for the bed upon which you rest, for the pillow. Nothing is too insignificant to be thankful for.

Name each blessing as your prayer of thanks, acknowledging Divine grace as the ultimate Source for all that is good in your life. This will open your heart and begin to re-bond you to God as a presence that loves and supports you. Quickly you will build a stronger spiritual foundation of trust, partnership and receiving. This will greatly amplify your capacity to serve and bless others with your love.

In the beginning you will probably feel silly. Cynicism may tempt you to revert back to listing complaints; but if you persist with gratitude you will find yourself drifting off to sleep in a state of real blessedness. Your dreams will be sweet, and you will find yourself waking in the morning feeling more positive and hopeful towards your life as a whole.

Morning gratitude

Work with this practice also in the moments upon awakening in the morning. As you lie dreamily in bed, direct your thoughts not towards planning the day or groaning about the fact that you must soon get up, but on opening your heart through appreciating that which you have. You might begin by thanking God for your partner asleep beside you, for your children in the next room, for your health or for the sun rising again of itself. This may sound sugary but do not mistake its power. Turning your energy towards gratitude will cause you to feel so much more energised, inspired, creative and alive. You will arise feeling more centred and connected with all that is.

Gratitude unlocks hidden gifts

As you become more skilful in the practice of gratitude, begin also offering thanks for the people and situations in your life that stretch you. Make the assumption that everything is occurring for your benefit, even if you do not know how. Choose to see everything as a gift, even if it is badly wrapped. Let your gratitude name your commitment to retrieving gifts from absolutely everything. In expressing gratitude for your difficulties, the armour erected between yourself and the solution dissolves more quickly. The wisdom with which to move forwards quickens its path to you.

The art of gratitude is to appreciate sooner rather than later. Gratitude is easy in retrospect, but more useful in the present. In reviewing my most difficult challenges, I can honestly say than everything has somehow contributed to me positively. Choosing to trust in that now shifts your life from struggle to flow.

The more you practise gratitude, the more it will begin to flood your waking awareness. Your eyes will be opened to the realisation that every moment is the most extraordinary gift from the cosmos to you, and your gratitude the beginning of your gift to it.

'If the only prayer you ever say is "thank you",
that would be enough.'

Meister Eckhart

12

Devotion:
being the Beloved

'Door of my heart
Open wide I keep for Thee.'

Paramahansa Yogananda

Within every human heart lies a yearning to draw itself into eternity through the mystic porthole of the love within you. Devotion is the driving force of this unconscious heart-wisdom. Cultivating it gives you access to experiencing Boundless Love, feeding you psychic nutrients to become more consistently loving towards all life.

Devotion is the virgin space in the heart that no affliction can destroy. Within it lies the essence of who you are, whole and eternally innocent. It is the ancient song of love that all life sings to you all of the time, even though you may have become deafened to its music. Devotion is the acknowledgement that you have heard this song, and desire to consciously re-bond with it, that your whole life may dance with its sublime and happy music. Devotion is the wordless celebration of what your heart loves and knows to be true beyond all else. Devotional practices thaw out a heart that has grown numb from too much hurt.

Imagine opening to an awareness of being completely, unconditionally, rapturously loved just for existing. If you were to profoundly register that God is totally devoted to you:

* How would you feel?
* How would you think?
* What would drop away from your life?
* What would emerge in its place?

God is beyond conception yet intimately near. Although absolute reality is transcendent and impersonal, all mystic traditions speak of an imminent and deeply personal face of God. Sufis call this 'the Friend', Christians the 'Holy Spirit'. Tibetan Buddhists related to this as 'Tara' or other Bodhisattvas, Hindus as 'the Divine Mother', mystic Jews as 'Shekinah'. Devotion is the language of this imminent aspect of God, which gives itself wholly to you and loves you passionately. That is why mystics often speak through poetry, dance and song. Everyday language is inadequate to transcribe such Boundless Love.

The love of God is broader than the measure of the mind. It cannot be grasped by logic, it must be sensed by more subtle antennae. When you tune into your soul's deepest longings, you recognise that the Divine embrace is what you have always craved.

The mystic doorway of devotion

Devotion is a central pillar within every ancient system of spirituality: Jewish prayers of praise and thanksgiving, Christian prayer and worship, Islamic salat (five times daily prayer), Sufi zikrs, Hindu bhajans, Buddhist pujas. Sages have universally emphasised that any sincere act of devotion awakens the dynamic power of love.

There is an ancient Sufi saying that, 'I am not the one who loves in me. It is the Beloved's own love that loves the Beloved in me.' At the highest level, devotion is the breath of love itself, loving through you. Giving your energy and commitment to that which resonates most within your heart, separation dissolves.

Consciously joining with that which permeates all things helps you harvest the wisdom of your vast heart. Devotion makes everything easier because it dissolves feelings of frailty. It makes the universal spiritual directives of kindness, acceptance, trust and forgiveness possible and practical. Working with devotional practices has given me powerful feelings of being:

* **Supported:** Knowing you are unconditionally loved helps you know that wherever you go, all life rises to support you.
* **Inspired:** As the heart re-bonds with heaven, the mind is inspired with clarity and new vision for the way ahead.

* **Creative:** New life always comes through some form of joining, and abundant ideas flood the one who has joined with the
  Source of all life.
* **Blessed with infinite resources:** Joining your heart to the heart
  of everything gives you the means to transcend limitations.

Many years ago I counselled a client called Annette who experienced a radical shift through a practice of devotion. When
Annette first came to see me, she was one of the most withdrawn
people I had ever encountered. Depressed and deeply shy,
Annette had little to say, other than to tell me that there was no
love and no hope in her life. She had no recollection of when her
inner light seemed to have gone out. For three months our weekly sessions felt like pulling teeth. No psychological approach I
tried seemed to have any impact.

One day Annette arrived for our session in such a dramatically
different state I wondered whether she had discovered hallu-
cinogenic drugs. Annette described an experience she had
received in a guided meditation of absolutely knowing that God
loved her. Not remotely a religious person, Annette opened to
something profound that warmed her at a core level. This filtered
through her whole being. Mentally, Annette gained a new perspective on difficult history with her parents, a fresher attitude to
her working life, and a significantly more hopeful way of relating
towards herself. Emotionally, she evolved a new ability to share
herself and be reached by others. Physically, her perpetual tired-
ness gave way to energy. Through opening her heart to receive
Divine love, Annette gained vision and meaning.

The remainder of our work together focused on helping
Annette recognise that this experience was not a chance occur-
rence, but one that could become an unfolding experience
through the practice of devotion.

The dynamics of devotion

The love between parent and child is often the purest and
strongest love we know. In those deeply sweet moments when a
young child says spontaneously to its parent, 'I love you', the
parent's heart opens to allow an increased surge of love back to

the child. This occurs in spite of the parent's human limitations or inability to express love. The natural order of things is that parents love their children. No matter what the story, this primal bond runs very deep. Multiply human parental love by a thousand and you are getting close to the level of love the Divine has for you.

Irrespective of all that you believe yourself to be, you are a child of God. When you open up what the Hindus call the bhakti (devotional) spirit within, offering your gratitude and love with simple child-like passion, a new awareness is born. An inner mystic doorway opens where you become available to receive the grace of Boundless Love. Experiencing a love beyond conception, your soul begins to sing with wordless gratitude and joy.

This has power to change everything. Receiving God's love shines new light into your life. As your love and devotion grows, the darkness within and without diminishes, revealing more of the truth of you Boundless Self. The prophet Mohammed said, 'Take one step towards God, and God will take a thousand steps towards you.' However, the deeper you go into devotion, a vision of unity unfolds whereby distinctions of 'God' and 'self' become unreal. Do not try to think it through too much. Remember that devotion bypasses logic. Just turn within to the powerhouse of your heart. There your soul's yearning to come home into Boundless Love will lead you into a whole new world. Your past sufferings will begin to melt into a deep peace.

Be not afraid of love

What could be more natural than love? Yet what are we often most afraid of? These are the fears I have encountered in opening my heart up to devotion. See which resonates for you.

* **Independence:** So accustomed have we become to 'doing life on our own', that the idea of yielding to a higher element can seem like a loss of power or Self. Ask for help in letting go of inappropriate independence and replacing it with Divine inter-dependence.
* **Unworthiness:** Often we feel unworthy to receive the level of love the Boundless wants to give us. Ask for help in letting go of unworthiness to become a better receiver.

* **Lack of faith in yourself:** Often when despondency kicks in we can sabotage ourselves from even trying something that may really help. Ask for help in letting go of this faithlessness and opening to new possibilities.

* **Belief in a punishing God:** This mistake is very deep, and the residue of fearful theology highly toxic. Ask for help in letting go of the idea that God is anything other than a universal force of total love that supports you.

You will discover that no matter how far you may have wandered or for how long, Love is all that waits for you. Loving arms are open to you irrespective of your fears and mistakes. You can return to your true home at any moment. Why not now?

A devotion practice

⤶ Sit in your sacred space. Light a candle and place before you something that inspires within you the feeling of being blessed – a picture of your child, of someone you deeply love, a beautiful flower, an object or symbol of the form of the Divine you relate to.

⤶ Keeping your eyes open, take whatever time you need to centre yourself. Let your breath deepen and the muscles in your body relax a little more with each exhale. Unhook from the day's events to relax and calm yourself. If it feels comfortable, place both hands over your heart.

⤶ Look upon the symbol of blessedness before you. Breathe in and let the feeling of gratitude well up in your heart. As you exhale, let your heart pour out-wards towards the source of this blessedness – thank you. With each inhale let the feelings of blessedness expand within your heart, and with each exhale let that beam your gratitude, as though you are pouring your whole being towards heaven.

⤶ Close your eyes, and reach even deeper into your heart to find the inner place beyond gratitude where there is just deep love. On the exhale, pour your loving devotion to the Divine, as though from somewhere deep inside you are calling to God, wordlessly saying, 'I love you . . . come to me.' On every out-breath, reach out from your heart to the heart of the eternal.

⤶ On the inhale, breathe in all the love you have given, returned to you a thousandfold. Drink it in through your heart and let it infiltrate your entire being.

_◢_ Breathing out – offering your wordless love . . . breathing in – receiving God's love for you. Breathing out – pouring your devotion . . . breathing in – drinking in the Divine . . . . Notice a growing feeling of unity, oneness, interconnectedness . . . . Let the breath breathe you.

_◢_ Let yourself be re-bonded with the heart of everything. Let scintillating light illuminate your vision. Let there no longer be two beings . . . just light within light, love within love, unity unfolding itself in perfect harmony and peace.

_◢_ When you are ready, bring this experience back into everyday awareness, as you gently stretch your body and slowly open your eyes. Stay seated for a few minutes to help you integrate your experience rather than switch off from it.

Everyday devotion

The famous musician Van Morrison was once asked in an interview: 'For whom did you write the beautiful love song *Have I told you lately that I love you?*' He replied, 'For God.'

In the Hindu tradition such 'Bhajans' – love songs to the Divine – help develop the bhakti (devotional) capacity within everyday activities. An easy and enjoyable way of opening your heart to greater love and devotion is to sing your favourite popular love songs as you go about mundane tasks, singing them to God, or to the Divine in your loved one. Learn to relate to God as your beloved, your closest friend, your ultimate confidant, the one you trust completely. Then you will come to know that God's grace is closer to you than your own heart.

May your heart forever be open to receive the knowledge of how profoundly loved you are.

13

Joining: the bridge to unity

'The sole purpose of all spiritual endeavour is to abolish the distinction between you and I.'

Sri Anandamayi Ma

Soon after I was ordained as an Interfaith Minister, I was invited to a function honouring peace-making projects organised by a theology department of Oxford University. It was a formal, conservative and male dominated gathering held at a gentleman's club in Mayfair, London. This was the first time that the club had allowed women through its doors. I was the youngest there by at least 20 years. The welcome was cordial but not exactly warm.

Not really knowing anyone, I set about introducing myself and joining in conversations. I said hello to a gentleman I remember having briefly spoken to at a conference six months prior. He was a larger than life character in his later years. His demeanour suggested a life of rank, privilege and a few too many years in the army. At first he did not remember me, but when he did, bellowed with a voice that could have deafened a football field, 'You're the one who nearly gave me a heart attack last year', and then launched into an outrageous professional assassination of the project I had just begun. It was one of those horrible moments where you wish the earth would open and swallow you.

Amidst such an onslaught, it was clear that to justify myself would be futile. To emerge from the encounter unscathed I had to choose the more yin – feminine – approach of joining rather than defensiveness and counter attack. Outwardly I listened as he voiced his scathing opinions, and inwardly I prayed for help in directing my focus to the highest truth within us both: that which is beyond the kinds of judgements his personality was making and beyond my feelings of offence.

I opened my heart to make contact with the truth of his heart, searching for the point of oneness underneath our differences, and inwardly reminded him of our – his and my – innocence, wholeness and right to be respected and loved. Through my heart I non-verbally spoke to him, 'I honour you as my brother and my friend. I behold the truth in you that I may know the truth of my self.' I began to notice that as I held this focus his aggressive attitude began to soften and he began to ask genuine questions about my work. He listened attentively as I answered. By the end of our 10-minute exchange he had dramatically turned around. Our conversation ended with him booming words of praise at me, 'I think it's jolly marvellous what you're doing and I think we need a few more about like you.'

It was a powerful lesson in the practical power of joining – that a non-verbal bridge to a more peaceful unified experience can be built through the heart even when two people have diametrically different backgrounds, values and points of view.

What is joining?

While devotion is a vertical movement of love between you and God, joining is a method of re-establishing an awareness of unity horizontally between people. If the core problem in any situation is some form of separation, resulting in fearful, defensive behaviour, joining provides a heart-centred way of dissolving it by focusing on the highest truth until all that remains is peace. Joining is a form of spiritual empathy driven by an active intention to love. Joining is the choice to make soul contact, and to keep making that choice even when contact may appear to be dangerous or impossible. Joining diffuses defences because, at core, all defences are a call for love and acceptance. When loving contact is offered, there simply is no further need for walls.

Whenever you reach out from the truth in you to connect with the core essence of another person, you experience God. Joining at the soul level is the choice from one mind to another to make heart-to-heart contact beyond the personality, the body and behaviour. Through the heart, communication is at its most direct.

Soul level joining brings deep comfort and a feeling of coming home. It ends loneliness because it dissolves the mistake of separation. Joining reminds us that we are not meant to walk through life alone, and that life is richer, sweeter and more meaningful when it is shared.

Joining helps resolve human conflict, helping us to find psychic common ground, even when we appear to have nothing in common. Joining paves the way for true communication when we cannot seem to reach one another. Joining helps us see illusions for what they are, and helps us celebrate the unity and wholeness that is the ultimate truth of our being. Joining breathes new life into our soul and helps us heal one another of old wounds. Soul level joining breeds authenticity, intimacy and makes way for love.

What to join to?

I have spoken previously about the two primary drives within every human mind: the Ego Self and its drive for separation and fear, and the Boundless Self, with its drive towards unity and love. The Ego Self, being a thought of separation, can never truly join, but it does attempt forms of pseudo joining. For example, the ego is often willing to 'join in' with another person's fearful perspective, their desire to attack and defend, their negative patterns and poor sense of self. Joining with people on this level is undesirable, is not genuinely supportive to anyone, and will pull you away from your centre.

Get conscious in your joining. Choose to join others in the vision of hope, even when there appears to be none. Join them in the vision of wholeness, even in the midst of old wounds. Join them in limitless possibility when they appear to be facing a wall. Join them in innocence in the face of mistakes. Join them in having faith in the goodness of life, people and themselves. Most of all join them in love. The art of joining is this: join with whatever you want strengthened. Whatever you join to, you draw towards yourself.

Joining is reaching out from the highest in you to the highest in others. It is often the case that the simplest and most direct means of experiencing the Divine are met with the most resistance. Remembering that joining is not sacrifice and that you are never asked to join with someone's painful behaviour, only the truth of their soul, ask yourself, 'Where and with whom may I be unwilling to join? Why?' Some common reasons for unwillingness to join include:

* Preserving your old defences.
* The need to be right or in control.
* Addiction to pain and struggle.
* The need for superiority.
* Confusion that joining equals powerlessness.

In a wounded state, gaining a 'victory' over another can take precedence over joining. Whatever resistance you discover, remind yourself that fighting for dominance only ever perpetuates power struggles – never ends them. Where there is a fight, there is no peace. Joining lays loving tracks for breakthroughs.

Behind unwillingness to join, there is fear of joining. Ask yourself, 'Where and with whom may I be afraid to join? Why?' Typical fears are of being dominated, losing control and losing your Self. Remember that losing is not joining, it is sacrifice. Once you have named your fears of joining, the only way you are going to know they have no foundation is to take the plunge and test it.

A joining meditation

The following is an easy joining meditation. I use it whenever I have a communication difficulty with someone, or am finding it hard to connect with someone I love. I have shared this method with countless parents who have found it especially helpful in reaching a withdrawn, angry or upset child.

⤺ Sit comfortably in your sacred space. Turn your focus inwards towards your heart and take a few minutes to let go, relaxing a little more with each exhalation. Let the gentle rhythm of your breath help you enter into a space of calm . . . .

⤺ Call upon the Divine to help you come into the remembrance of your Boundless Self. Ask, 'Bring me into my highest truth.' Sit with this request and breathe into the area in your heart until you feel it begin to expand, soften and open in love. Feel a quiet power emerging from within you . . . .

⟶ Choose someone with whom you would like to make a deeper connection, some healing or a breakthrough. Trust that whoever comes to you will be the most appropriate person for you to work with.

⟶ See their face up ahead of you, feel into their presence and into your feelings about them, hear their voice. Be willing in your mind's eye to reach for the highest within them. Brush past their difficult personality traits and behaviours, your history together and your fears of deeper contact with them to search for a seed of light in their heart. Trust that although it may be shrouded, it is there.

⟶ Once you can see this seed of light, reach out from your heart to this seed of light within their heart and walk towards it. Let the light within both of your hearts form a bridge of grace.

⟶ Let this light draw you forwards towards the highest in them, with your heart wide open. Pour into them whatever you would most like to receive: respect, love, appreciation, acceptance and what you sense is their true need.

⟶ Give freely, knowing that everything you give you give to yourself. Let go of your sense of yourself as a separate body and feel into the place of oneness. Speak to them the contents of your heart, your intention to honour them and regard them as your equal, your willingness to see them for who they truly are, and other wordless words of love and remembrance.

⟶ Let all fears, and everything but the truth of who you both are drop away. Notice as you join in the highest truth, a greater sense of your authentic self emerges, accompanied by feelings of release and happiness. Enjoy this. You have simply returned to the reality of your true relationship with this person, and the true reality of your Boundless Self.

⟶ Wish for this person all good things, and take your time returning to the awareness of where you are by taking a few deeper breaths, having a stretch and opening your eyes. If you do this practice regularly – preferably whenever you feel your heart close down to anyone – you will come into the awareness that in truth you have always been joined. The practice of joining then becomes a means for remembering what always has been, and always will be.

'Each time someone enters your mind, think of them
with your heart open and extending, even if it is only
for a few moments. They will prosper, blossom, be lifted up,
feel loved and know they have value. So will you.'

Lency Spezzano

Metta: loving kindness

'In life, three things are truly important:
The first is to be kind,
The second is to be kind,
The third is to be kind.'

Henry James

The most fantastic experiences are often the simple little moments when we drop our defences and connect with one another in the spirit of kinship and kindness. Life is beautiful when our highest priority is love.

I cannot remember exactly when I first learned the Buddhist practice of metta – loving kindness. However, when I began to take the practice seriously it utterly transformed my inner experience and the way I operate within the world. I have shared this practice with counselling clients, students, friends and family members, moving through all varieties of human issues. I have never seen it fail to make a powerful positive impact in the life of anyone who sincerely embraces it.

Metta practice purifies the human heart by cleansing it of selfishness, hatred, anger, judgement and fear, which are the primary causes of dis-harmony. Metta cultivates your inbuilt capacity for soul empathy and understanding. It is the perfect antidote to the fearful, self-centred mind-set that so drains modern western culture. Nothing could be a more powerful contribution to the world than cultivating a kind heart.

The word 'metta' comes from the Pali language and has two root meanings. The first is 'to be gentle'. Metta has been likened to gentle rain that falls upon the earth. The rain does not select where to rain and where to avoid rainfall, rather, it falls without discrimination. Similarly, the goal of loving kindness practice is not just to offer blessings to those who you find it easy to love and meet your expectations, but to learn to embrace all beings everywhere with the same degree of loving kindness you would offer your lover or child.

The other root of 'metta' means 'friend'. The Buddha described a good friend as someone who is constant in times of happiness and in times of adversity, and who would not forsake you when in trouble nor rejoice in your difficulties. A true friend is a helper who will care for you when you are unable to care for yourself, and a refuge to you when you are afraid. The goal of metta is to become such a friend to all of life.

All of the mystical traditions speak of the principle that giving is receiving. To give truly, whole-heartedly and without posting an emotional invoice is to taste our unity and receive unbounded blessings. The Ego Self confuses real giving with sacrifice. Believing that love is finite, the ego assumes giving means we personally go without.

As we give from our hearts, the opposite occurs. Just as waves on the ocean are unique from one another, yet form part of the whole ocean, so each person is unique yet intimately inter-connected with the whole. When you truly register your oneness with all life, all giving is a gift to yourself. Working with metta to become a gentle friend to life, life begins to become a gentle friend to you.

The gifts of metta

Replace self-hatred with happiness

Your core essence is Boundless Love, but this easily becomes clouded by fears and old wounds. Heartbreaks can seem to remove you from your innocence and wholeness. This leads to self-hatred and low self-esteem, which form the cornerstone of dysfunctional patterns and sabotage mechanisms.

Metta practice intelligently begins by firstly cultivating loving kindness towards yourself before attempting to offer it outward towards others. Offering kind blessings within oxygenates and heals your deepest wounds and brings you into closer contact with the truth of who you are. In this way stagnation gives rise to greater wholeness and happiness. For most people, this is the most difficult stage of the practice.

Heal narcissism and self-obsession

High stress levels, imbalanced life goals and unresolved wounds from the past can easily lead you into forgetting the most important things in life. Your perspective narrows when you are stressed, making it is easy to become selfish and dissociated from your own heart and the hearts of others.

Metta practice insists that your personal freedom, peace and happiness are indivisible from that of others. Consciously offering blessings of loving kindness to others re-connects you to the spirit of generosity, which injects a more balanced and compassionate perspective into life. When you cultivate compassion for another, your own suffering eases.

Initiate healing in difficult relationships

Inevitably there will be people in your life who you find it difficult to like, let alone love, and people who find you equally as difficult. Although communication is vital in building good relationships with others, sometimes it feels impossible to navigate through your differences when hurt and angry. The fourth stage of metta practice aims to go beyond the personality and reduce the issue to its most basic level – all human beings want, need and deserve to be loved and accepted.

Metta asks for your willingness to move beyond the 'right or wrong' behaviour to build a bridge to higher ground. Instead of seeking 'justice', which frequently masks a desire for revenge, metta focuses on giving the love that is required. This begins to initiate a change of perception within your own being. Often it also produces a psychic opening within the other person. This has the power to completely alter the dynamics of a relationship.

Help lift depression

Having suffered from depression myself, I firmly believe that depression is a spiritual sickness, and that spiritual perspectives and practice of some kind are a pivotal part of full recovery. I once had an interesting conversation with a psychiatrist who said, 'The soul seems to shrink when depressed.' I responded, 'Perhaps it is because we allow our contact with the soul to shrink that we get depressed.'

Two of the central dynamics of depression are the feeling of immense separation and aloneness, and the feeling of having no purpose or value in life. Learning to connect from the heart and give your love addresses both your deepest need and your highest purpose. No matter what your outward vocation may be, the spiritual vocation of everyone on earth is to learn how to love well. I have witnessed metta practice literally open up a whole new world for people with depression.

The practice of metta

The following is the version of metta that I have been working with for years. If the prayer grates with you, create your own based around the basic sentiments of wishing peace, happiness and freedom from harm for yourself and others. When meditating upon loving kindness, always follow the sequence of blessing yourself first, then someone you care about, then a neutral person, then someone you find difficult, and finally all beings everywhere.

✐ Sit in your sacred space. Close your eyes, consciously relax the muscles in your body. Focus on the gentle rise and fall of your breath. Sink inwards towards your heart.

✐ Breathe into your heart as though your breath is fanning a tiny flame of light – the flame of loving kindness. Try to feel this flame as a feeling of love, tenderness and kindness welling up inside you. Let each breath empower the flame of loving kindness, the same way as oxygen encourages a fire to catch light. Feel your heart softening, expanding and opening . . . .

Loving kindness towards yourself

✐ Reflect upon your own basic goodness; your desire to love and be loved. See yourself as a little child, whose basic wish and right is to be happy and at peace. Imagine enfolding this child in a tender embrace, and say slowly to yourself this blessing prayer:

May I dwell in the heart
May I be free from suffering
May I be healed
May I know my wholeness
May I be happy and at peace.

✐ Sit with this for a few minutes or as long as feels comfortable. Visualise pouring love and blessings into the image of yourself as a child. If you wander, return to bless yourself with the warm intentions of the prayer.

Loving kindness towards a loved one

⟞ Call to mind someone you care deeply about. Reflect upon their goodness, your love for them, your wishes for them to receive abundant blessings. See their face before you and visualise holding their face tenderly in your hands as you look into their eyes and say from your heart to theirs:

> May you dwell in the heart
> May you be free from suffering
> May you be healed
> May you know your wholeness
> May you be happy and at peace.

⟞ Pour your love and desire for happiness into them. Bless them with all you have. Sit with this for a few minutes or as long as feels comfortable.

Loving kindness towards a neutral person

⟞ Turn your mind to someone you regularly come into contact with but do not know intimately. Perhaps it is the face of a shopkeeper or someone you remember passing on the street. See the vision of their face before you and visualise yourself reaching out to hold their face tenderly in your hands as you offer the highest love possible to them. Say with great tenderness:

> May you dwell in the heart
> May you be free from suffering
> May you be healed
> May you know your wholeness
> May you be happy and at peace.

⟞ Pour your love and desire for their happiness into them. Bless them with all you have for at least a few minutes.

Loving kindness towards someone 'difficult'

⟞ Turn your mind to someone who challenges you, someone you feel has hurt or threatened you, whom you are upset or angry with. Mild annoyances count!

⟞ Your anger does not bring you peace. Instead, it keeps your wounds alive and holds you back from inner freedom. For your own sake, be willing to offer the same loving kindness towards them that you offered your loved one – whether you believe they deserve it or not. See their face before you and be willing to look through your judgements of them to see their basic goodness and right to be happy, regardless of what they said or did. Be willing to see the light beyond your experience of them as you say from your heart to theirs:

May you dwell in the heart
May you be free from suffering
May you be healed
May you know your wholeness
May you be happy and at peace.

⤇ Pour your love into them. Be willing to bless them with all you have. Stay with this for at least a few minutes.

Loving kindness to all beings

⤇ Let your heart expand further to let your love and care flow to encompass all beings everywhere. Begin blessing the people in close proximity to you, those you live with, your neighbours, those in your town, your region, your country, neighbouring countries, neighbouring continents . . . . Visualise a wave of unconditional love flowing from your heart to the hearts of all beings in the world, wishing for them the basic right of happiness, freedom and peace.

May all beings dwell in the heart
May all be free from suffering
May all be healed
May all know their wholeness
May all be happy and at peace.

Everyday metta

There are whole communities of people across the globe practising metta – concentrating the vast power of the heart to radiate blessings to all beings. Know that at any time, someone somewhere in the world is sitting in metta meditation blessing you, wishing you heart-centredness, freedom, healing, wholeness, peace and happiness. May this knowledge both hold you in your difficult moments and inspire you to contribute similarly.

Whatever you do today, whoever you speak to or meet, bless them with your loving kindness. Speak silently the metta prayer to their heart. Be their soul friend. Know that in doing so you have contributed to a less violent, more loving world.

'Sustaining a loving heart, even for the duration of the
snap of a finger, makes one a truly spiritual being.'

The Buddha

Tonglen: the miracle of compassion

'If I am not for myself who will be?
If I am only for myself who am I?
And if not now, when?'

Rabbi Hillel

The degree of your compassion is the true mark of your spirituality. Tonglen is a powerful Tibetan Buddhist practice that helps transform suffering within yourself and others. It expands your natural capacity for compassion and causes you to grow in love.

An old friend whom I had lost touch with ten years ago looked me up on my last visit to Australia. Michelle and I had been close in our late teens and early twenties, and bonded over our passion for spirituality. She had always been so vivacious, energetic, and passionately alive. We met up on a hot summer's day under a huge Karri Tree in Kings Park, Perth. 'Tell me all about your life now?' I asked her. Hearing that Michelle was fighting a malignant brain tumour, recovering from the trauma of four major operations and the most recent bout of radiotherapy was the last thing I expected to hear.

Tears streamed down Michelle's cheeks as she told me her story: years of intense pain, uncertainty, extreme side effects of aggressive medication, difficult responses from family members, and her struggle to find peace. Michelle then looked right into me and said, 'The worst thing in all this is that I feel so alone.' Friends had been extra kind for the first few months, but seemed to keep their distance now that she is unable to 'be positive' and is not getting better.

Sitting with Michelle I knew that the last thing on earth she needed in that moment was my advice. So, far more important than words could be, I joined with her and gave her my heart for a couple of hours. I did my best to be absolutely present and non-resistant to her reality. I listened to her anger and despair as she repeated many times 'I am not ready to die.' I felt into her pain and loneliness and amidst it saw great courage, spirit and humour.

In spite of her dire medical prognosis I chose to focus on seeing Michelle as a whole being, not as a cancer-stricken body. I held faith that somehow, though I know not how, she would find peace. Joining with Michelle in the whole gamut of her experience did not drain me; on the contrary, it left me feeling humbled, honoured and deeply blessed. It left her smiling, laughing and feeling human again. We had connected where it matters most.

Your compassion heals separation

Suffering hits you twice. First, in any trial you have to deal with the sickness, heartbreak or trauma itself and, second, the sense of loneliness, fear and separation it produces. Suffering deepens the illusion of absolute aloneness. More potent than any medicine, your own loving presence is the spiritual cure.

We may not have the power to bring back to life a mother killed in an accident for her grieving son, or magically cure a friend of cancer. However, we can develop the ability to stay present and keep our hearts open that the burden of fear and pain may be somewhat lightened, or at the very least, not faced alone.

We need to accept the fact that life in a body contains some inherent difficulties. This is Buddha's first noble truth: that life contains suffering. His solution to this problem of suffering is to awaken from our dislocated sense of self and the cravings it produces through spiritual practice. Whatever path you choose, while you identify with your Ego Self, experiencing some sickness or heartbreak at some point in your life is inevitable. Suffering does not discriminate.

There need be no judgement or shame about the fact that you have an ego and hence some difficulties. However, it will help enormously if you can utilise suffering – yours or another's – to grow in acceptance, surrender and love. Approached in this way, the greatest trials can midwife the priceless gift of a vast heart. This would be enough to begin dissolving the fear, mistaken identity and sense of separation that is the ultimate cause of all suffering.

Every time you extend yourself compassionately to anyone, you let go of another layer of attachment to your Ego Self, and cleave a little more to your Boundless Self. Every call to compassion you respond to develops within you the higher skills of love, taking you closer to the truth of your being. To respond lovingly to another's suffering is to reduce your own.

Focus on loving not fixing

We live in such a 'quick fix' society that often when confronted with a difficult situation that has no obvious solution, our heart numbs out. We can become irritated with the lack of change or we just exit. This happens because we mistake fixing for loving. When our fixing fails to work, feelings of helplessness confront us.

Helplessness is a form of overwhelm where you seem to reach the limitations of your personal resources and believe you have nothing more to give. You withdraw from another for fear of being dragged down into the black hole yourself. This can only ever happen when you rely on the resources of your separate Self.

The alternative to withdrawal when you feel helpless before someone's suffering is to join your heart with the vast heart of God. Consciously connecting to limitless resources of grace enables you to just be present to that person and let the compassion extend through you. Inner wisdom will guide you in what to do. When you connect to the source of all healing, there is no need to resist suffering.

Next time you hit helplessness or fear of being swallowed up and are tempted to withdraw, re-source in the awareness of your Boundless Self. Call upon Divine compassion to breathe through you. Remember that the person before you is whole, despite how broken they may appear. People feel deeply loved and supported when they are seen for who they are, not simply the state they are in.

Just open your heart

Compassion isn't just a method, it is being present and giving your whole heart the way that God would. I discovered this at a whole new level when I became carer to my husband Robert who experienced a serious spinal injury. For six weeks Robert was in constant pain and unable to move. The GP failed to diagnose him properly and give the medication to cope with such extreme pain. I navigated my way through endless conventional and complementary health practitioners to get Robert the treatment he needed just to be able to sleep. Amidst this, my heart broke open to levels of love and compassion I had never known before. There was nothing that I would not do to alleviate his pain, yet little I could do in actuality. Paradoxically, it was an excruciating yet strangely graceful experience.

As a result of this experience I felt even deeper empathy with others. Their pain was my pain. My heart went out at a whole new level to anyone I heard about who was suffering in any way. Instead of bringing me down, it raised me to levels of humility and gratitude I had never experienced before.

During Robert's crisis, some friends were exceptionally loving, and others gave us well-intentioned new age interpretations, such as, 'Robert obviously needs to address his support issues', or, 'Where is he going wrong to have this happen?' Such comments really got under my skin. In my meditation room one day, I questioned whether I had ever displayed such ignorance, giving 'platitudinous healing' to someone in their time of need. Realising that I had, I wrote a prayer of apology to every friend or client to who in some subtle way I had tried to fix or lacked patience with. Embarrassed for having given subtle platitudes, or simply lacking the faith to stay present and give the compassion and vision that was truly required, this was a huge turning point for me.

That is when I came back to working with the practice of tonglen, which I had been taught many years before at a Buddhist retreat. The basic premise of tonglen is that you first centre yourself and then, as you breathe in, visualise 'opening to receive' the fear, sadness, distress or loneliness you confront in yourself or others. On the out breath, 'give out' all love, peace, healing, light, faith and hope. Being in complete non-resistance to the suffering and giving pure love in return is mighty alchemy.

Contact can never contaminate you

Your ego will counsel that tonglen is essentially dangerous, yet your spirit knows it has power to free you from your own suffering as well as transmute the suffering of others. It is completely safe because although everyone experiences their suffering as very real, it is founded in the illusion of separation. Nothing born of an illusion can contaminate your true essence.

In the light of our spiritual oneness, allowing yourself to connect with the suffering of others and also with the highest truth in others brings the realisation that there is no such thing as 'your pain' and 'my pain', or 'your truth' and 'my truth'. There is simply the collective Ego Self and the collective Boundless Self.

The practice of tonglen

Sit in your sacred space and close your eyes. Turn inwards and let calmness come. Breathe deeply and let the muscles in your body relax.

Ask inwardly to be brought into your deepest centre, into contact with the vast heart of God and the truth of who you are. Feel a beam of brilliant light anchor you to this awareness of yourself . . . .

Take as long as you need until you feel centred here.

Tonglen for yourself

Imagine that in front of you stands an image of yourself: the part that suffers or struggles, that fears, feels guilty, inadequate, small, frail or alone. Staying anchored in your centre, open your heart towards the small sense of self. Do not judge or resist it. It calls for your loving help.

On the inhale, 'breathe in' this self, as though breathing in wisps of black clouds. Let the vast heart with which you are bonded absorb and transform it. As you exhale, 'breathe out' pure light, peace, love, kindness and healing given you by the vast heart of all. Keep breathing in the suffering, letting the heart transmute it, and breathe out the healing qualities that are needed.

Tonglen for another

↙ Call to mind someone you know is experiencing difficulty. Visualise them before you, open to the whole range of their experience and 'breathe in' their feelings; the fear, struggle, sense of lack, distress, pain. Imagine it as wisps of black cloud coming into your heart, where it is absorbed and transmuted into light. 'Breathe out' all the love and healing qualities that are needed. Most importantly, see them as whole, not as their difficulty.

↙ Keep doing this for as long as feels comfortable, then return to the sense of yourself as being wrapped up within the heart of compassion itself.

Tonglen for all beings

↙ Now open your heart to encompass all beings everywhere, including those in 'trouble spots' around the globe. Do not be afraid of contamination as you 'breathe in' all the suffering, fear, anger and grief of the world. Trust that the vast heart of God can handle it and allow light, peace, love, trust and faith to extend out of your heart to the hearts of all. Let compassion breathe you.

↙ Keep doing this as long as feels right, then return to just resting within your open heart.

Everyday Tonglen

Whatever you encounter today, do not resist it. Perhaps you are here to help transform it. Ask for help in anchoring within your Boundless Self, and 'breathe in' the presenting pain or fear. 'Breathe out' its opposite – peace, love, trust, joy. Keep your heart open in the face of everything. Consciously bond with the vast heart of God and grace will emerge. Trust that the sting of suffering will be lifted somehow.

'Past the seeker as he prayed by the river came
The leper, the destitute, the war-torn and the heart-broken.
He cried to the heavens: "How is it that a God of love
Can see such things and do nothing?"
A soft voice replied: I did do something,
I sent YOU.'

Sufi story

Part V

DIVINE MIND

16

Breath: oxygen for the soul

'Breathe and attain one-pointedness.
Then the harmony of heaven
Will come down and dwell in you.
You will be radiant with life.
You will rest in Tao.'

Chuang Tzu, Taoist sage

Breath is the mechanism that allows the subtle forces of life to flow through you. It has the power to relax your body, release old stress, calm your mind, foster spiritual concentration and bring you back into the present moment. It also helps you retrieve the gifts of your Divine mind.

I first discovered the transformative power of breath in my early twenties when I trained in Rebirthing. The simple method of conscious connected breathing, taken from an ancient yogic method, impressed me with its capacity to shift old pain, fear and trauma. I would not have believed the states of spiritual clarity and bliss a simple breathing method could evoke unless I had experienced it myself.

Your breath really can breathe you past illusions back into your Boundless Self. This is not a new revelation. Spiritual systems around the world have used the breath in various forms as a vital meditation tool for centuries. Breath is the most universal method for cultivating mindfulness – coming more fully into the present that you may live it fully. Taoists, Buddhists and Yogis have long regarded 'prana' or 'chi' – the life force within the breath – as the 'vehicle of the mind'. In mystical Judaism, each breath is regarded as 'ruah', the sacred emanation of God itself that infuses all Creation. Christian mystic texts overflow with references to the 'breath of the Holy Spirit', and contemplative meditations around the prayer, 'Breathe on me breath of God.' So intrinsic is the breath to Sufi and Taoist meditations that practises excluding it would be unimaginable.

It is a common trap to believe that spiritual awakening must be complex. Breathing strips meditation back to its raw essentials. They are:

* Learning to let go.
* Learning to be with what is.
* Letting the truth shine.

In simply learning to let the breath of life breathe you, these three universal lessons of ceasing to cling to the old, non-resistance to the present and opening to welcome the truth can become practical living realities.

Still your mind

A student asked the great Hindu sage Ramana Maharshi,'What stands in the way of my knowing my Self and God?' He shot back, 'Your wandering mind.' To still the mind is a difficult but important task. In our culture of over stimulation we are developing ever-poorer attention spans. Concentration is the precursor to pure being.

If you could learn to relinquish fears and outer stimuli and not resist whatever you discover in the present, your mind would become still. All of the natural gifts of God would shine upon you. You would realise that every true need is fulfilled. There would be nothing to fear and every question would be answered by inner wisdom. What stands in the way of this experience is the internal chatter of your mind. Working with your breath can help calm it.

Everyday ego chatter keeps you from being present to the love that is here now, and keeps hidden the true thoughts that extend naturally from your Divine mind. When your mind is still and present, it is free to flow with love, wisdom, kindness, compassion and other emanations of your eternal wholeness. A tranquil mind is an enormous gift.

Under the ego's authority, the body and brain is a doing machine. It is always moving on to the next thing. I am not suggesting you aim for no thought – that would be impossible to hold for long in the body – but aim for quieting fearful thoughts and learning to welcome back your true thoughts. These are thoughts you think in alignment with God. You will know them by their absence of fear, harshness, judgement, complaints and criticism.

Try this experiment

Close your eyes and simply watch the thoughts in your mind for three minutes. Do it now . . . .

What thoughts did you notice? Did you discover yourself making mental shopping lists, re-viewing your finances, re-hashing yesterday's conversations, planning tomorrow's activities, wondering whether others will like you, whether you will be good enough or whether you will meet your deadline? Essentially, you would have seen a preview of your fears about yesterday and your fantasies about tomorrow.

No effort, no trying

Sinking into meditation via the simplicity of your breath could help to unwind these distractions. As the mystic author Andrew Harvey describes, 'Imagine that you and all your worries, fantasies and fears are like a large lump of butter left outside in the sun.' Butter left in the sun will slowly, effortlessly melt. Do not fear that you will dissolve. What dissolves as you sit, breathe and be is the chatter, the fears, false identifications and clinging. Your essence remains, and is then freer to shine.

Just breathing, returning to the present moment and letting distractions melt away makes you clearer, more aware and more sensitive to shifting thoughts and emotions, but without becoming washed away with them. As Native American elders beautifully taught, you learn to 'be with' your emotions, not become them. This translates into greater peace and awareness in everyday life, strengthening your capacity to transform the habitual patterns and reactions that can so easily trash your life.

Create breathing space: a meditation

There are many ways of meditating with the breath. Each method has its own specific purpose. The approach I share here is designed to help you sink into stillness through mindfulness – being present. It is simple, yet if practised regularly can produce great clarity and calm. Although this practice is more than potent enough in itself, it can also serve as a wonderful preparation for prayer and other forms of inner practice.

Sit in your sacred space and close your eyes. Imagine that your body, your thoughts, your concerns are like that slab of butter in the sunshine . . . . Feel as though you are melting inwards . . . melting into the now. Relax . . . .

Become aware of the natural rhythm of your breathing. Notice the cool air at your nostrils as you inhale, and the warm air in front of you as you exhale. Notice the sensation in your lungs as you breathe in and out . . . . Your breath may naturally slow, deepen and become more rhythmical, but do not try to control or force it . . . just melt, letting your body and mind relax and let go that little bit more, as you rest with the simple miracle of breathing in and out.

Pay attention to your experience exactly as it is. Sink deeper and deeper inwards, being with the gentle rise and fall of your inhale and exhale.

Inevitably, as you focus on just breathing and being, distractions will come. Do not resist them. Just keep coming back to melting and breathing. Let it all be part of your experience. Your thoughts will run away to noises outside the room, an itch on your leg, and distracting thoughts of yesterday and tomorrow. This is perfectly natural. Do not judge or condemn yourself for getting distracted.

If you drift off you may find it helpful to take one long, deeper breath and then return to breathing naturally. You will get more out of the meditation if you bring yourself gently back to the breath. Just keep breathing, melting into what is. Eventually the breath will breathe you into pure being. There is no need for any striving whatsoever.

If this brings up difficult memories to the surface, take it as a positive sign: your psyche is ready to release old hurts. Just pay attention, melt and keep coming back to the breath. If you do not resist them they will release quite naturally.

✍ To come out of the practice, simply open your eyes and continue the practice with your eyes open for a minute or two. Take a few deeper breaths if you like and have a stretch. Move slowly into your activities. This will help you integrate the calm you have gleaned in silence into the day's activities.

Breathing space within everyday actions

* **Remind yourself at intervals through the day to breathe:** It encourages you to move with whatever is occurring rather than tensing up and resisting it. Resistance equals stress.
* **Aim to do only one thing at a time!:** This is not as impossible as it may sound. When preparing breakfast – give yourself wholly to that and just prepare breakfast. When speaking on the telephone, relish the person and the conversation you are having and just connect wholly with them. Trying to do several things simultaneously fries your sense of centre. Remembering to breathe and be as present as you can to whatever is happening makes you more efficient, less dispersed and infinitely calmer.
* **When you come unstuck (and we all do) just stop:** Make re-connecting to peace in the present more important than anything else you may think needs to be done. Remember that lump of butter in the sunshine and just breathe and melt into now. The solution will come much more quickly when you relax. I promise!

'Breathing in, I calm my body
breathing out, I smile.
Dwelling in the present moment,
I know this is a wonderful moment.'

Thich Nhat Hanh

17

Mantra: singing into silence

*'The mantra becomes one's staff of life
And carries you through every ordeal'.*

Mahatma Gandhi

My early forays into meditation as a teenager were discouraging affairs. I had to accept that my mind was more scrambled than my eggs at breakfast. At the time I had little discipline and even less patience. The practice that really helped to cut through the clutter and lift me out of my inner emotional chaos was the use of a mantra. Simple Sanskrit mantras given to me by my yoga teacher at the time were enormously calming, centring and powerful in their ability to anchor me quickly into greater silence.

Nearly 20 years on, I still turn to mantras and sacred singing when I need help in concentrating and quieting my mind, when I feel my inner power plug to Boundless Love has become too loose. The Hindu Gayantri Mantra and the simple word AUM, which I was given as a teenager, together with the Hebrew mantra 'Adonai li, v'lo ira', which I was taught in seminary by Rabbi Joseph Gelberman, still nourish me today. I have found mantras and sacred singing help to de-hypnotise my mind from its old cravings, projections and attachments, opening me to know the strength, energy and peace of the Boundless Presence that pervades all things.

Tap into Divine power

Using a mantra involves singing, speaking or silent inward recital of a name of the Divine, taken from a combination of sacred syllables from ancient languages. The Hindu Upanishads describe an eternal primal sound that rings from the heart of existence. This is thought to be the sound of God. Rishis, the wise seers of old, tuned into this sound and translated it into audible rhythms and words. These are known as mantras. Because of such origins, each syllable of an ancient mantra is thought to carry the living power of the Absolute. Many mystics believe that working with a mantra can help form a nucleus of spiritual power with which to access grace directly. Whether or not you believe this, I have witnessed mantra practice producing noticeable positive changes within thousands of clients and students. Using a mantra is deeply calming.

Steady your mind

The primary purpose of mantra is to help steady the mind by giving it something constructive to focus on. Sacred singing is used as a primary focal point within every spiritual tradition, whether it be Christian hymns and monastic chants, Jewish cantorials, Islamic calls to prayer or Hindu Bhajans. Mantras are particularly prevalent within Sufism, Buddhism and Hinduism and within these eastern traditions, devoted recitation of an ancient mantra is seen as the fastest way of transcending the surface mind's distractions and entering the depths of the spirit where Boundless Love glows eternally.

Despite its esoteric origins, mantra practice is so simple a child can do it. In whatever circumstances you find yourself, singing a simple sacred phrase or name of God with dedication and passion in the depths of the heart can unify your faculties. Gathering you into a more cohesive whole, mantra practice helps shoot your awareness back into God.

Like the hush following the ring of a meditation bell, mantra initiates a deeper silence. Utilising the will through repetition of the mantra, the feelings through the devotion that mantra will evoke, and the senses through enforced deeper breathing and sound resonance, mind, emotions and body are calmed. When these usually active faculties are quieted, the whole being is concentrated and a deep silence can emerge.

Heal beyond the intellect

Using a mantra is subtle, potent medicine. Every time you sing or say a name of the Divine you cleanse a veil of your ego thoughts of fear, anger, vengeance, hatred, selfishness and ignorance. The heart is opened and blockages within the subtle spiritual centres can gradually release. This leaves a little more space for trust, love, kindness, wisdom and joy. To evoke God is to evoke your Boundless Self. With this comes your higher thoughts and true being. Mantras help refine and rededicate your mind, heart and body so that more of your true nature can shine.

Something miraculous occurs when the intellect is suspended. Sigmund Freud once said that, 'Intelligence will often be used in the service of the neurosis.' Mantra helps by-pass the kind of intellectual gymnastics that often cause unnecessary obstacles in the meditative process, fostering deeper surrender.

Although Western science is only just beginning to explore the healing power of sound, our instinctive natures have known that singing and uttering ancient lyrics stirs something within the soul when words themselves are not enough. Mothers naturally sing to soothe their young children, communities sing together to unify the collective spirit and every country sings a national anthem to raise patriotism. Sound is like lyrical poetry that penetrates where rationality cannot.

Bond with ancients' wisdom

I have noticed an interesting phenomenon in my years of leading groups and that is that whatever breakthroughs and awareness are achieved within one group they seem to spill through into the one behind it. Each new group seems to stand energetically on the shoulders of the previous one.

The same dynamic occurs when you embrace an ancient mantra as opposed to creating your own. The power, longing and devotion accrued through millions of seekers who have employed it comes to bless you. Its power is enhanced as you gain the energetic assistance of those who have come before you. Mantras are living gifts from the ancients to you.

Sing yourself home

There are thousands of mantras to choose from. The small handful I share with you here are simple, powerful and from varied sources. To begin with, try chanting each one, paying attention to the response each mantra evokes in you, and choose intuitively whichever feels most resonant and meaningful. Unfortunately I am not able through the written word to share the melodies I was taught to accompany these mantras. However, there are so many variations it would not hurt to let your own musical instincts take charge.

Once you have chosen a mantra it is best to stick with it rather than chop and change. In that way you can let it go to work on you. Please do not be intimidated! These mantras are simply sacred sounds to help carry you into silence. Take your pick.

* **OM** (pronounced A-U-M): The foundation of all Hindu and Buddhist mantras, this is powerfully calming and centring. AUM is considered to be the cosmic primal sound itself and if such thing could have translation it would probably be 'pure being, consciousness, bliss'. Brilliant for lovers of simplicity.
* **Adonai li, v'lo ira** (pronounced adonay lee velo ira): In Hebrew this translates as 'God is with me. I will not fear.' It is exceptionally comforting, strengthening and calming.
* **Maranatha** (pronounced Ma-ra-na-tha): Aramaic mantra of the early Christian Desert Fathers, which was outlawed in the Middle Ages because of its potency, Maranatha translates as 'O Lord, come.' This mantra feels very intimate.
* **Om Nama Shivayah** (pronounced Om na-ma she-vay-yah): A Hindu mantra to Shiva, Lord of birth and re-birth, this is a powerfully healing and purifying mantra translating as 'I bow to the truth – please destroy my ignorance.' It is great for cutting through old patterns.
* **Om mani padme hum** (pronounced Om manee padmeh humm): This is the Tibetan mantra of Avalokiteshvara, the Buddha of compassion, and means 'All hail to the jewel in the heart of the lotus', or in western speak, to the Boundless Love consciousness that waits to be uncovered within every being.

* **Allah** (pronounced All-ahh): The Arabic word for God used in Sufi practice. This can feel deeply tender and intimate, so is best suited to those with a devotional nature.

Working with a mantra

Having chosen the mantra that most appeals to you, here are some pointers to help you work with it. A lovely tip from author Andrew Harvey is to sit somewhere quiet and begin by praying to all beings who have used this mantra before you to help infuse you with its sacred truth.

Close your eyes and place your two palms over your heart as you begin to recite the mantra. I find this simple act deepens my experience of the mantra enormously. Do this if it feels comfortable and begin to recite your chosen mantra out loud with each exhale, singing it if you like. Do not worry if you feel weird doing this – everyone does at first. Just keep singing or saying your mantra in the way that feels most natural and meditate in your heart on its meaning.

Saying the mantra in different ways will produce different effects within you. Singing the mantra powerfully lifts the spirit, opens the heart and calms the body's nervous system. Saying the mantra out loud steadies and focuses the mind, and whispering it can help usher in a new sense of Divine intimacy. Experiment and go with your instincts as to what you feel you need.

When ready, let the mantra trail off and just sink into silence. Let go and feel as though you are falling into the essence of the mantra . . . into vast spaciousness.

You can use this deep silence as a springboard for prayer or Divine dialogue, although the silence of pure being is often the deepest prayer. To come back, think not of exiting the meditation, but bringing its gifts forward into your day. Open your eyes, stretch and begin to move into simple activity, and as you do so, inwardly repeat the mantra.

Mantra within daily activities

Hindu sages guided their students to, 'Keep the mantra spinning amidst all your activities.' During mechanical duties such as emptying the dishwasher, cleaning the house or taking the dog for a walk, you can recite your mantra to help keep your mind focused and clear throughout the day. However, use your common sense. Do not recite your mantra when you should really be giving your full attention to your activity, such as driving. If you are ever in doubt about the appropriateness of reciting your mantra, take this acid test. Ask yourself, 'Is reciting my mantra helping me be more present, open, centred and joyous in what I'm presently doing?' Don't be a space cadet – you can fly high but stay grounded in what's important. Also, 'Is saying or singing my mantra respectful to others in my immediate vicinity?' Opening to Boundless Love means being mindful to your neighbours, never imposing your practice onto them.

As you keep singing your mantra, you will become aware that the Divine song is singing you. In truth, it always has, and forever will. You will come to the realisation that your mantra is the song you sing with God.

'Listen, listen, this wonderful sound
brings me back to my true self.'

Thich Nhat Hanh

18

Centring prayer

True prayer is not haggling with Heaven
It is aligning yourself to Heaven.

David, a company director and devoted father of three, was going through a very painful divorce. A spiritually minded person, he was horrified at the depth of his anger towards his ex-wife. Frightened of losing his kids, David became his worst self around her. Awash with endless strategies of revenge and control, his ego mind was working over-time, and all of his plans for a better life were backfiring.

David's psychology had failed him. I suggested the most practical step he could take right now would be to pray. He looked scared. I suggested that if he could find a bridge to his higher mind, he would be freer from his own reactions that so got in the way. 'Centre yourself first and the clarity you need to respond appropriately will emerge', I promised.

I taught David two methods of centring prayer that I share with you now. Sceptical but willing, he tried them and instantly noticed a difference. He became less afraid and more peaceful. He gained greater clarity, which gave him the capacity to communicate honestly without attack. Three years later, David is thriving, on amicable terms with his ex, and using centring prayer daily to keep grounding his mind in his Boundless Self.

Pray first, act later

A spiritual principle that I have found so deeply helpful is Jesus' teaching to, 'Seek ye first the Kingdom of Heaven and all else will be added unto you.' Usually when faced with a situation that feels frightening, we try to resolve the outer problem before coming to God and to our own spiritual centre. We make the mistake of thinking that once we've attended to all our tasks and problems, then we can pray.

In rushing to fix the externals we overlook the internal cause of all problems: we have wandered from our centre, and thus lost love's vision. This spawns every mistake, unkind word and inappropriate action. The beginning of every resolution is to return to inner peace. Centring prayer is a wonderful method to help you do that.

Centring prayer evolved out of ancient mystic Christian monastic approaches to meditation. It offers an approach to re-connecting with grace and higher wisdom through calling upon the Divine name that is most personally meaningful. It is a beautifully simple method to plug your mind back into your true source of strength.

Although in reality you have never actually been disconnected from God, you are prone to regularly forget the strength of your spiritual home. This causes you to lose contact with your Boundless Self and your true mind. This forgetting leaves you feeling unnecessarily frail, frightened and alone.

Centring prayer is the opening of your heart, mind and whole being to the experience of Boundless Love, within which is your true Self. Whenever you call upon the name of God that resounds in your heart, illusions fall away. Repeat God's name, which contains the highest truth about you and all beings, and cravings and false desires drop away much more easily. As you call upon the highest there is, your rightful inheritance of strength, peace and love returns to you. Returned to your natural state, clarity emerges for the practical way forward.

Repeating the name of God and of your true Self is like erecting a pillar of light through your entire being. The Name becomes to your mind, emotions and spirit what a strong spine is to your body. As with mantra, calling upon God's name purifies your mind, raises you out of fear and returns you to wisdom once more.

> *'Say God's name, and you invite the angels*
> *To surround the ground on which you stand,*
> *And sing to you as they spread their wings to keep you safe,*
> *And shelter you from every worldly thought*
> *That would intrude upon your holiness.'*

A Course in Miracles

Call upon your God

True prayer has little to do with the actual words you say and everything to do with the feeling and intention behind them. Whatever is uttered from the depths of your being is heard loud and clear. Choose a name of the Divine that is meaningful and holds maximal emotional impact for you, for example: God, Goddess, Mother, Father, Love, Jesus, Krishna, Shiva, Allah, Adonai, Tara, Holy Spirit, Beloved, Self. Perhaps ask inwardly what the best name for God is for you to work with. It can be any word that signifies the Absolute for you, but it needs to be a single word.

The name that you choose then becomes the rope that carries you to your Divine mind. Use it as a springboard into silence. Let this name become the all-encompassing idea that holds your mind completely.

Fall into your centre

Now that you have chosen the name of God to anchor your mind, take it into a short meditation using these instructions inspired by my friend and spiritual teacher Robert Perry.

Sit comfortably and close your eyes. Sink inwards and draw your attention within. Begin to call the name, slowly and intentionally, over and over. Synchronise it with your exhale if you like. Put your focus on the name and relax into it.

Repeat your name for God as an act of calling the Divine to come into your awareness and experience. Expect to be heard. Expect a response.

Now repeat the Name as a way of calling on the awareness of your Boundless Self, and the clarity, wisdom, love, joy and peace this Self contains. By calling on God you call upon your true Self, for they are one.

Repeat the Name now as a way of calling upon all reality, including the reality of all people and beings, for they too are one with God.

⤺ Now repeat your name for God as a prayer that asks for peace of mind and everything you truly want, a prayer of your heart that contains all possible prayers.

⤺ Now repeat the Name passionately from the place of your deepest yearning – as a dart of longing love.

⤺ Let all these meanings blend together into one, so that by inwardly reciting the Name you call upon everything real and everything you truly want.

⤺ When your mind wanders to something besides the Name and the feelings of serenity it brings, just return to focus your mind by gently repeating the Name. This may mean you are calling on the Name fairly constantly. That is fine. Repeat it as an affirmation that peace of mind is more important to you than the thing you were thinking about. Meditation teachers universally agree that you will get more out of the practice if you bring yourself back to the Name instead of indulging in mind wandering.

This practice makes for a most beautiful morning meditation, but can be used anytime, anywhere as a simple way to bring you back to centre as often as you need. The more frequently you use this practice, the stronger a response you will feel. Over time, you will feel as though light and peace is bursting forward from within your mind.

Everyday anchor prayers

Just as a captain puts down an anchor to prevent his boat drifting away, so your Name for God or a short phrase becomes the anchor to keep your mind rooted in a place of calm. Building on the same principles as calling God's name, anchor prayers are simple, emotionally grounding one-liners that are the closest I come to affirmations. The basic premise is this: anchor yourself in the highest truth and all that is not authentically you falls away. I encourage everyone I work with to use them because they are so practical in the midst of busy lives.

Where affirmations utilise a positive statement to train the mind towards a positive goal, anchor prayers call upon Divine reserves to ground your highest intention. Anchor prayers back your willingness to open to what is with grace. Anchor prayers and centring prayer can be used:

* In silence as a focal point for meditation.
* Upon waking and going to sleep.

* At various intervals throughout the day.
* As a response to fearful thinking, difficulty and stress.

Personally, I find that using anchor prayers as a response to fearful thinking is second to none. As with calling upon the name of God, the key to success lies in creating prayers that have the most meaning and emotional impact for you. You may want to look to your favourite inspirational text for help with this, but first consider:

* What emotions most frequently steer me off course? (Is your emotional Achilles heel one of anger, fear, insecurity or lack?)
* To keep my mind connected with my Boundless Self, what do I most need?

Your anchor prayer should speak directly to your need. Here are some of my favourites. Use them as a base to create your own.

* 'I rest in God.' *A Course in Miracles*
* 'Lead me from the unreal to the Real.' *The Upanishads*
* 'Breathe on me breath of God.' Hildegarde of Bingen
* 'Be still and know.' Julian of Norwich
* 'There is nothing but God.' Sufism
* 'May I awaken from forgetfulness and find my true home.' Thich Nhat Hanh
* 'Let me look on all things through love today.'
* 'Help me remember that nothing is beyond me.'
* 'Help me give to all beings what I want to receive today.'
* 'Love, lead my way.'

Prefix your anchor prayer with your name of God. In addition to your intention, you evoke the power and strength gleaned from the intimacy of your relationship with the Divine. Know that there is no difficulty that your willingness and the Boundless Love of God together cannot shift. Prayer truly is the medium of miracles.

> 'Lead me from the unreal to the real
> Lead me from darkness to the light
> Lead me from death to immortality
> Om shanti shanti shanti (peace).'
>
> *The Upanishads*

19

Moving into stillness

'To a mind that is still
the whole universe surrenders.'

Chuang Tzu

Years ago I came across the most beautiful sculpture in a public garden. It was a large stylised depiction of a woman sitting peacefully. Although carved in stone and inanimate, for me that sculpture was totally charged. It spoke to my deep love of stillness and the all-pervading experience of pure being. Whenever I enter deep stillness, an un-nameable joy stirs within me. Amidst that vast spaciousness, stripped of everything except my essence, I feel truly my Self, truly at home.

Stillness is often mistaken for lazy idleness. Where idleness is sedentary and passively asleep to the wonder of now, stillness is dynamic. Stillness is available when the physical senses are quieted and the chattering surface mind is calmed. In stillness, the spirit can soar and the eternal can reign. In stillness, Boundless Love is all that exists. Your essence and the essence of all creation rests within it. The peace is indescribable.

Although stillness is the purest language, it is often the most difficult to learn. While your Boundless Self is naturally still, the noise your Ego Self makes is relentless. Constantly striving for the next thing it promises will make you feel whole, it is never content with what is here now. That is why all approaches to meditation use a focus to dive underneath the ego mind into truer states of being.

When my mind is distracted and bound up in its own tense knots, I find some form of movement helps me enter deep stillness. Not throwing myself around at the gymnasium, but mindful movements that fully involve my every faculty – body, mind and intention. It seems contradictory, but movement can help usher you past distractions into stillness.

Dive beyond the senses

In the course of any Interfaith Seminary gathering, we pray, dance, sing, breathe, laugh, explore and be still. Engaging as many dimensions of our being as possible, not just our minds, takes the experience of whatever subject we are exploring that much deeper. Any time the group hits resistance, saturation or a level of stuckness, we move. Sometimes I put on some music and invite everyone to close their eyes and dance. Other times we stand and shake while naming out loud our fears or doubts. Other times we use body prayer, taking a simple prayer or mantra and 'praying it' using simple movements with our bodies. Whatever form of movement we choose, there comes a point where the chaos gives way to something else, sometimes something truly extraordinary.

All of the mystical traditions understood the relationship of movement to stillness. Buddhist monks of every lineage use walking meditation to develop mindfulness in action. Hinduism developed Hatha yoga as one part of a comprehensive system to focus and balance the senses so as to ready the practitioner for deeper meditative practice. The Chinese developed methods such as t'ai chi and chi kung for concentrating and stilling the inner subtle forces. Indigenous cultures all used dance as a way of entering deeper states in ritual. Muslims pray Salat (five times daily prayer), with their body, and for many Sufi orders prayers are put to music and movement.

Movement creates oceans of spaciousness

While you are not your body, but a spiritual being having a physical experience, fighting your way into stillness when tired, overwhelmed or frustrated is silly. There will be some days when it is relatively easy for you to just sit quietly, turn within and be still. Other days you may struggle with it. In these times, you may find it easier to first give yourself wholly to some kind of movement until resistance subsides. Five rhythms meditation creator Gabrielle Roth describes this as 'sweating your prayers'. Then deep stillness can become like a soft cushion to just fall into.

If you live or work in a city, the chances are that you spend much of your day sedentary, starved of oxygen and nature, and assaulted by harsh sights and sounds. Such environmental stresses can make it harder to find stillness unless you consciously counteract them. Moving into stillness is especially helpful if you have a kinaesthetic dominance, in that wisdom speaks to you through feeling sensations in your body. What's more, movement is good fun.

Aside from the physical benefits of exercise, movement benefits your inner being in many ways. When approached with an intention to be whole-hearted and present, movement can help you to:

* Move stuck energy.
* Focus and re-energise.
* Integrate when feeling full up or overwhelmed.
* Shift negative states.
* Ground you in the present moment.
* Throw off the stress of the day.
* Create inner space.
* Get out of your own way.
* Let go.

Jeremy, a marketing consultant and close friend, is one of the most spiritually committed people I know. Deeply humble, he had undertaken at least an hour a day of contemplative meditation for many years. A few years ago, seemingly out of nowhere, old, intense feelings from childhood emerged that despite his awareness he could not find a name for, let alone move beyond. Jeremy felt locked-in emotionally and physically, deeply frustrated and angry with himself.

Jeremy began to work with more dynamic forms of meditation, from vigorous shaking to chi kung exercises, then dropping into stillness. To his amazement he discovered new levels of freedom, clarity and grounding. He received so much from this approach that movement-based meditation has since become the mainstay of his practice.

Move into calm beyond thought

Like water, which can clearly mirror the sky only so long as its surface is undisturbed, the mind can only reflect your true Self when it is tranquil. Movement is a great way to cut through mental clutter. In diving wholly into movement you are brought full circle. The ego mind stops pushing and starts to flow. In letting go, grace appears naturally.

Here are some approaches to moving beyond inner noise through movement that work well for me and those I have shared them with. Do not force anything, but the more wholly you give yourself to the movement the deeper it will take you.

Shaking

Find a space where you can move undisturbed. Light a candle and dedicate your movement to finding deep stillness, and begin to shake your body. Begin by shaking gently – moving your arms and legs, and working your way to shaking your whole body strongly but not violently. As you shake, imagine shaking off your doubts, your fears, your insecurities, your anxieties . . . whatever you want to let go of, shake it out. Trust that the shaking and your intention will create the space to move you beyond your inner obstacles. Let go and allow your body to really vibrate. Do this for at least five minutes, preferably fifteen. Then stop, sit and drop into stillness.

Dancing

Find a space where you can move in private near a decent stereo system. Choose some music that inspires you but that has no words that your mind can grip onto – either something in a language you do not understand, some African drumming or something instrumental. This is not the time to indulge your MTV rock star fantasies! Devotional Kawali music is fabulous, but if you can't think of anything, rousing classical music works well. Light a candle if you wish and dedicate your dance to dancing into stillness.

Turn your music up loud, close your eyes and let your body do whatever it wants to do. Try to let go of any notion of what your dancing should look like. Be concerned only with listening to the music and letting your body move as wholly and as freely as you can allow. Let go into the dance. Do this for at least 10 minutes, longer if you like, and then stop, turn the music off and sink inwards.

Running or walking in nature

Running in nature is one of my favourite movement meditations, but running or walking on a noisy gym treadmill simply will not do. Part of the medicine is greenery, space and the life force that only nature provides. For me, the rhythm of a long gentle run clears my mind like nothing else, but you need to be reasonably fit to relax into it. If you prefer something less intense, walking will work also. Be present to each step, the sound and feel of each breath, the environment around you, and to let go into it.

Dedicate your running or walking to the undoing of inner noise, and try to find a path away from busy roads that will be supportive of that intention. Pay attention. Inevitably your mind will wander and get bored and, when it does, just bring yourself back to the present moment: each step and each breath. Alternatively, you can internally recite a mantra or name of God as outlined in previous chapters to focus your mind on your goal. When you are ready to stop, wind down gently, stretching whatever you need to stretch. As soon as you possibly can, come to sit silently. Just be still . . . .

Body prayers

Body prayers have been a beautiful revelation to me in recent years. Their power and grace have been awoken in me largely through Nina McGhie, a recent Interfaith Seminary graduate. Nina is an extraordinary dancer who has been almost completely deaf since birth. She communicates to the world through movement. Whenever I led any kind of prayer or practice in the groups, Nina would tune in her refined subtle senses and dance what she felt. Her presence stimulated me, and indeed the whole group, to pray our deepest intentions not just with words, but with everything we have.

Take a simple prayer that speaks deeply to you, one that is easy to learn without having to be read. You could use a mantra or anchor prayer, or even better, write your own prayer. Take some time to reflect upon what each word or sound means, and intuitively let your body find its way to express it in gentle movement. Once you have found the movement that feels right, pray the prayer with your voice, your heart and your body. Do it over and over, giving your whole being to it. Give the prayer your all, and let it move you. It will organically become quieter until words fall away and the body is just praying with movement. The moment to just stop and be still will find you. Enjoy!

Everyday stillness

You can use shorter versions of these practices to help relieve the build-up of stress and re-centre throughout the day. Whether you wish to use these methods, or find a good movement meditation teacher, remember to:

* Do the movement intentionally.
* Give yourself wholly to it.
* Set your intention beforehand for the movement to take you into deep stillness.

'Be still and know that I am God.' *The Psalms*

Be still and know that you are God.
Be still and know that all is God.
Be still and know . . .

Part VI

HEALING THE BLOCKS TO LOVE

20

Forgiveness: the key to freedom

If I were to offer you a spiritual tool which promised to:
* breathe new life in to all your relationships,
* open you to deep peace and happiness,
* improve your health in every way and
* free your Spirit,

would you try it?

Whatever the block, some form of forgiveness is the answer. My father taught me that. He could not have given me a greater gift. I was 18 when I first began to take forgiveness seriously. For years I had been carrying immense pain around my relationship with my father, whom I tried to distance myself from. We had always had an extremely difficult relationship. I experienced his behaviour as tyrannical, hurtful and damaging, and I blamed him for my own unhappiness and low self-esteem. Although committed in my spiritual practice and making many positive strides in my life, I still felt traumatised, powerless and blocked by this relationship. I relegated it to the 'too hard' basket.

I was on yet another weekend personal development course when I first heard the idea that forgiveness was the gift you give yourself: the key to personal freedom. I was told that, 'Any grievance you hold will sabotage your success, peace, happiness, health, relationships and life.' I felt resistant and hopeless. The idea of extending love towards my father filled me with fears of becoming a doormat for repeat performances of painful treatment. That was a prospect I was not willing to face. The 'homework' I was given from that workshop was to try to reconcile with him.

I was so caught up in fear and powerlessness that I wrote off my car in a head-on collision on the way home. The shock and injuries from the accident gave me a legitimate excuse not to meet up with my father for a while. 'Besides, now I had no means of transport.' To my unconscious mind, killing myself was an easier prospect than facing Dad. I had a dramatic case of resistance to forgiveness.

I justified to myself that forgiveness was fine for those who were genuinely remorseful, but not for those who deny the pain they cause and continue to injure. No matter how far I distanced myself from my father, the old patterns kept following me around. Even on other continents I seemed to have an uncanny knack of attracting people into my life who left me feeling utterly worthless, just the way my father had. I realised that these festering past issues would continue to re-present themselves in different guises until I had resolved the pain. Intuitively, I knew forgiveness was the way forward. I played half-heartedly with the teaching for several years, without fully understanding what forgiveness really was.

Grievances block Boundless Love

I realised that I could not remain a victim and be happy. If I wanted to create and sustain loving relationships and inner peace I had to let go of my grievance. I committed myself wholeheartedly to do whatever it took to free myself of the painful dynamic I had with my father. I had absolutely no idea how I would achieve this, but I set it nevertheless. It was something I knew I needed to do for my own wellbeing.

I had always identified myself as the victim and he as victimiser, and felt powerless and locked in. I knew I had to find a way to feel and articulate my feelings, which I had denied and suppressed for so long. I began writing 'completion' letters to my father, trying to express myself. The initial letters were full of hurt and rage, so I kept writing and then burning the letters until I was ready to move on. I was so grateful for my few close friends who encouraged me to keep going in this cathartic stage.

The letter I eventually sent my Dad expressed my feelings in a much calmer manner, along with my intention to significantly improve our relationship. Even so, they were really letters of phoney-forgiveness. The undertone still said, 'In order for me to be at peace you need to change.' Although I was more aware of my feelings and better able to articulate them, I was still subtly blaming him for my struggles and limitations. Although I felt freer in myself and had gained more understanding of his behaviour, it did not produce the reconciliation I was after, because my fundamental intention had not changed.

Confusing effort for genuine willingness, I moved on to writing affirmations. I would write, 'I now open to a healed and healthy relationship with my father' a hundred times a day. This might have worked had I not the automatic unconscious extension of that affirmation in my mind saying, 'Only if he changes the way he treats me.' For a while it seemed that our relationship had improved and all my inner work had paid off, but it wasn't long before all the old patterns and destructive behaviours between us resurfaced again. I was yet to understand that real forgiveness makes no demands.

Blame never works

When the hurt and rage re-emerged, this time more intensely than ever, I was convinced that a showdown was the only viable option. I confronted my father with an ultimatum to either admit that his behaviour towards me was hurtful and damaging and be willing to seek help with me in resolving it, or to sever his relationship with me. He chose the latter.

I had no idea how to move forward from the depth of rejection and heartbreak that followed. What do you do when the one you struggle with denies your experience and is unwilling to engage in resolution? It took great honesty for me to realise that my intention had not really been to heal through forgiveness but to point the finger of blame. However justified my blame seemed, it was holding both of us hostage. I began to realise that I had been trying to push for reconciliation before I'd walked through the gate of forgiveness: that it worked the other way around.

I could understand the background to my father's behaviour towards me – that he was simply repeating the painful patterns of his unresolved childhood issues, but I had not been able to suspend my judgement of him to see beyond his behaviour to his essential core. It was only when I had exhausted all my options that I was willing to try God's. I realised that to forgive you must look through a different lens than the ego's.

Go beyond the story

Immediately after we married, Robert and I begun doing the workbook lessons of A Course in Miracles, a modern psycho-spiritual text whose central teaching is radical forgiveness. As instructed we read a lesson a day, and meditated on the exercises given. Something wonderful occurred on the day I reached the lesson Let miracles replace all grievances. This lesson instructed me to choose someone who I found difficult to love, someone whose name incited anger and fear, and go within to review the painful scenarios, reflecting upon the upset. In the face of so many seemingly good reasons to maintain my grievance towards my Dad the lesson instructed me to ask God's help in seeing him differently. It offered the following passage to meditate upon three times throughout the day:

> 'Let me behold my saviour in this one
> You have chosen as the one for me
> To ask to lead me into the holy light in which
> He stands, that I may join with him.'

At first I refused to do this lesson – it felt like an insult to everything I had suffered. However, my inner guidance, along with Robert's gentle support, said – just do it! So I sat for 20 minutes in that first meditation, holding my father's face in my mind, feeling all the pain I associated with our relationship, reviewing my wounds. My body was shaking and I felt sick, as my inner vision presented me with a monstrous exaggeration of my father's angry face.

I struggled with being asked to see the person who seemed to have caused me the greatest pain as my saviour, although I could accept that there was a higher purpose to this relationship. I had the greatest difficulty with the idea of joining with my father in light. My ego insisted that I was the spiritual one who held the moral high ground; that I stood in the light and he in the dark, which made joining impossible. Thankfully I had enough sense not to indulge my arrogance. I opened to join with whatever higher truth lay behind the father I knew, even though this was difficult and beyond the realm of my experience at that time.

The second meditation was much less emotional, more detached. I felt I was just going through the motions of the exercise, but I persisted anyway. On rising from the second meditation it occurred to me that perhaps there was a slight possibility that something could change. In the third meditation that day, the floodgates of my heart burst open and I saw myself, my father and our lives in a way I had never seen before – totally free of all guilt. It was as though loving hands peeled back the monstrous mask of my father to reveal the face of a young boy – in whose eyes shone the desire to be happy, to love and be loved. I could identify with that.

Now it was easy to join with my father's true essence behind the defences. I was not asked to condone any painful past behaviour, but rather to join with his highest essence and eradicate the need for any judgement at all. Visualising myself walking towards him with a completely open heart I was able to make soul contact and accept him fully. It was an exceptionally beautiful moment – tears streamed down my face in gratitude and release.

In seeing my father through different eyes, free of judgement and guilt, it became clear that he was, in fact, my gift from God. Through our difficulties I was forced to dig deep within myself for answers. Those answers walked me back into Boundless Love, into my true vocation at an early age, and gave me a depth of compassion that otherwise I could not have known. What I have had to learn in order to overcome these difficulties has gifted my life and the life of thousands of people more than anything else. Often, those who seem to present you with the greatest burdens are offering you the greatest gifts.

Communicate from your heart

After this powerful inner release I sat down to write my father a real completion letter – one that contained no blame, no subtle accusations and no demands for him to change. I simply re-stated my commitment to a loving, honest friendship where we both felt free. Additionally, I stated my willingness to take down my defences towards him. Seeing how much emotional barbed wire I had placed around my heart, defending myself against imminent attack, I realised how my defensiveness perpetuated the negative dynamic between us. Risky though this seemed, I stated my intention to lay down my armour completely and begin again. I discovered much later that as I took this stand for defencelessness, my father, on the other side of the world, independently decided for the first time in his life to obtain therapeutic support.

Six months after this inner shift, I met up with my father face to face. I prayed for help in holding the vision of my father's and my own innocence and for joining with the truth beyond our old story together. Having coffee with my Dad one morning I became aware that I no longer had to 'work' to keep my heart open to him. The old pain, fear and anger towards him had evaporated, leaving just profound gratitude, feelings of love, acceptance and sincere wishes for his happiness. The moment I shared this with him – completely unrehearsed and from my heart – was the moment I knew I was free. The past was gone.

A Course in Miracles states that, 'The holiest spot on earth is where an ancient hatred has become a present love.' This speaks most directly to me of what has taken place in my relationship with my father. In recent years, spending time with my father has become a whole new experience. I focus now on releasing expectations of how I think my father should be, giving him the freedom to be himself. Acceptance and self-acceptance are the guiding principles that make the relationship work. I am aware that we have an extensive history, but one that serves only to remind me of what's truly important. The past feels quite unreal. My perception has changed so radically, when I now look back upon my childhood, I remember many moments of my father's tenderness of which I had no previous recollection. Now, if any difficulty arises between us I am better able to communicate my feelings and hear his with greater honesty and acceptance, allowing us to move through any confusion more quickly and gracefully. As a direct consequence, every area of my life has moved to a whole new level of freedom and joy.

Grace can transmute the past

Forgiveness can work for you too. In my spiritual counselling practice I have worked with countless people facing all kinds of betrayal, abandonment, injustice, abuse, hurt and fear, and each has found the courage to open to profound forgiveness and reap rewards beyond their dreams. It makes no difference how difficult the issue, or how great the mistake or who made it, forgiveness is one of the primary gateways through which breakthroughs occur.

Forgiveness is love at its most practical. It is beyond effort and beyond psychology. Ultimately, forgiveness is an act of grace. For that grace to become active in transforming your grievances into gifts you must rise to greater levels of honesty, courage and faith. Forgiveness is simple, though not necessarily easy. Forgiveness asks you to compassionately recognise that your experiences, memories and feelings are perceptions not facts.

Forgiveness asks you to turn within and take complete responsibility for your experience, without blaming or condemning yourself for landing there. Forgiveness asks you to realise that what you judge in others is the projection of what you find intolerable within yourself. Forgiveness asks you to suspend your judgement of everyone and everything, to admit that you don't always see the full picture, and to remember that through spiritual vision there is a better way that will bring everyone concerned to true peace and safety.

Forgiveness gently reminds you that the guilt you see in another, which is just the reflection of your own hidden feelings of guilt, is a mistake and cannot obscure the majesty of who you and others truly are. Forgiveness returns you to the awareness of your wholeness, to the memory of our Oneness, to our collective reality as extensions of God and thus to sanity once more. In every moment, forgiveness gives you a clean slate in which to begin again. Right now, with the person you most judge, resist or blame, who most seems to hold you back, will you embrace it? Here's how.

The steps to forgiveness

1 Choose peace

Forgiveness starts whenever you want resolution more than you want the grievance. Claim your power to choose peace over being right, superior, in control, or holding the moral high ground.

✎ When you begin this step, you will probably notice that only a small part of you, say 10%, wants to choose peace, and the rest of you is screaming 'unfair' and wanting revenge!

✎ Let that be okay, sit quietly and keep repeating your choice inwardly, letting every breath raise your percentage of willingness bit by bit.

2 Feel your feelings

It is vitally important not to deny what you feel, or you just end up intellectualising rather than allowing true healing to occur. Indulging, justifying or dumping your feelings on anyone else will not help, but feeling your feelings honestly will.

✎ Extend acceptance to the parts of yourself that want to cling to the grievance. Don't deny or condemn yourself for whatever you feel but keep committing to real peace. Be kind to yourself within your difficult feelings. I offer more guidance on this in chapter 22 – Acceptance: embracing your Self.

3 Invite God in

Forgiveness moves through you, but is not of you. You do not need to know how forgiveness and healing will take place, just to be willing for it to do so.

✎ Ask to be shown how to see the other person as they truly are, and shown exactly what you need to see and do to free yourself.

✎ Pray – any time, any place, any how: 'Spirit, I give to You the way I perceive . . . now. I give You our relationship. Heal us both. I give You my defences. I give You my fears of love. I give You my fears of being free of this pain. Show me how to see past my hurts to the truth in [name] that we might both be free.'

4 Go beyond the story

Beyond what you know or don't know about the other person, the truth of who they really are shines in radiant light, completely untouched by any mistake. The truth of who they are remains as God created it, as does the truth of who you are. You are not asked to engage with unkind behaviour but to seek for that which lies beyond it. Claiming your own innocence depends on your willingness to see the seed of original innocence in another. The truth of who we are rests in unity.

✒ Take some time to sit quietly. Invite spirit to lead you in seeing a light ahead and a figure standing within that light. See yourself walking towards this light; the light of the truth about [name]. Walk step by step towards the truth in the other person with an honest and loving intention, and witness what you need to let go of to keep taking the next step.

✒ As you walk towards them, be willing to put everything else aside and pour your love into them, wish for them what you wish for yourself.

5 Trust the process

Be patient and know that your deepest intention will manifest in the way that is most appropriate.

✒ Be gentle with yourself when you hit resistance. Rest. Be still. Let go. Laugh often. Break out of your usual routine. Hang out with a friend. Keep your eyes and ears open – the help you have asked for will come.

6 Surrender

As you surrender old pains and old judgements, surrender also your fear of receiving the enormous amounts of energy, love, happiness, creativity and inspiration that will inevitably follow.

✒ Pray: 'Spirit: help me to receive the abundant blessings You have in store for me as I forgive and let go today.'

Be warned, miracles will follow!

'Who is the bravest hero?
He who turns his enemy into a friend.'

Talmud

21

Alchemical prayer

Beloved
I offer You my mind, my heart, my soul
My fears, my illusions, my yearnings, my all.
Release me back into Boundless Love.

Prayer is the bridge over troubled water that can ease your mind. Through prayer you gain access to a grace beyond this world that can deliver you out of painful bondage and into deep peace. Prayer is the most underrated, under-tried method of transforming obstacles, yet one of the most effective.

In my early twenties I began to work with an adapted form of 'treatment prayer' as taught in Science of Mind metaphysics. It showed me how to identify problems and their hidden payoffs in my mind, and hand them over to the Divine for healing. I was stunned at how directly and powerfully such prayers released me back into a more truthful awareness. Neuroses, limiting beliefs and fears evaporated more effortlessly.

Whenever I was aware of feeling afraid, inadequate or caught up in old patterns I would stop and pray in this way. My prayers were always answered by a feeling of greater peace. Prayer seemed to back my willingness to move forward with the might of Heaven. With such a potent tool I began to know that nothing was beyond my reach.

I have seen prayer turn around deep depressions, lift intense pain and transform many kinds of seemingly hopeless situations. Just as an airplane pilot continues to travel forward but seeks a higher altitude when encountering turbulence, so prayer helps you to find higher ground for the way forward when challenges arise.

John had been coming for weekly sessions for a few months.

A highly intelligent and sensitive journalist, he suffered from resistant depression. Fear, guilt and anxiety dominated his life. So tense he could hardly breathe, John's thought process was exceptionally negative. This had been going on for so long it had become a habit.

To prevent his fears escalating into such negative states, I shared with John a method I evolved out of the 'treatment prayer' model that I call alchemical prayer. Every evening John began to review his day and give to God anything he was afraid of or guilty about. He would give over his fears of letting go of his fears, and ask for help in opening to a more loving vision. John quickly grew calmer, more peaceful and more trusting. Regular practice empowered him with the awareness that he need not be a victim to fear and guilt. This made dealing with his underlying issues less frightening.

The ladder back to peace

All difficult, painful feelings come from having unknowingly taken a detour into a state of separation, where fear, guilt and lack reign. In this state, resources are limited and you lie victim to others' behaviours in the external world. As I have mentioned previously, the beginning of any resolution is the rising out of your Ego Self into your Boundless Self. Here, the wisdom, love and vision needed are available to you. Whether or not you remember having wandered into a fearful state, prayer acts as a re-set button, helping you to find your feet in love and trust again.

Even if you believe in a transcendent Divine presence, or Buddha nature within rather than a personal God, prayer calls that Presence into the forefront of your awareness. As you pray, your true nature becomes dynamic in your being. Rising into Love's boundless vision instead of your ego's limitations, your state shifts. Flow returns, and you feel lighter and more refined.

It is never God's will that you suffer, but the Boundless cannot help you with things you keep to yourself. That is why you must bring your darkness to the light to allow grace to release you. A loving God will never force or demand anything of you and will never violate your free will. Whenever you try to handle your difficulties alone, you perpetuate your own suffering and remove yourself from Divine help. Yet, should you change your mind and ask, Boundless Love will respond fully.

God's grace is a corrective force that is entirely free of judgement, therefore it is safe to give over even your darkest thoughts. Whenever you surrender your mistaken perceptions, beliefs, fear and doubts to the Boundless, grace clears the way for you. Common anxieties such as believing you are not good enough, feeling unworthy to receive abundant happiness, feeling unlovable, believing you need to prove yourself or thinking something terrible would happen if you failed to meet someone's expectations, are mistakes that call for correction. They contradict the reality of your wholeness and obstruct your true unlimited nature.

Muster as much honesty as possible about the true causes of your pain or block. The more specific you are, the better. Then raise your willingness to come back to peace, and yield yourself to God. Whenever you genuinely offer up your mistaken beliefs and fears they are untied like Divine nimble fingers untying a knotted ball of wool. In the light of Boundless Love, your illusions dissolve. You are released back into a truer awareness of your Self and what is. In undoing mistaken perceptions, flow, clarity and wisdom re-emerge.

Nothing is too great or small to ask for Divine help. This is the message that has been repeated by countless sages across the globe. The Koran invites us to, 'Call upon God for untying the lace upon your sandal.' Jesus directs his disciples to 'be as little children'. Children are not afraid to ask for insight when they do not understand. Do not content yourself with just a little less fear, God wants you to have complete peace of mind, a deeply sweet life and to know, give and receive Boundless Love.

The more you call upon God, the more substantially you will feel the power and the presence with you. Your capacity to receive will increase, and you will come into a deeper realisation just how profoundly abundant life really is. This will support every area of your life.

Just speak to God

Prayer need not be a particularly pious act, just a natural speaking to God of our intentions and yearnings. Many of us have become so accustomed to thinking we need to do everything ourselves that we forget to pray. The only way to remedy this is to weave prayer regularly into your life. When exploring Islam at the Interfaith Seminary I ask the whole group to aim to take five short daily interludes of prayer. Few actually manage it, but something truly extraordinary always occurs to those who give it their best shot.

Another common obstacle to prayer is pride: feeling a failure if we can't resolve problems by ourselves. Some feel foolish or believe they do not know how to pray. Someone once revealed to me their block to prayer in difficult situations was that if the prayer failed to work then they had exhausted their final option. My close friend, spiritual teacher and author Diane Berke, describes prayer as a 'come-as-you-are-party'. It is as simple as just bringing whatever you struggle with and talking to God about it as openly as you would talk to your dearest, most trust-worthy friend.

The Tibetans have a wonderful proverb that, 'There is nothing so feeble as actions without prayer.' Too often we use prayer as a last resort – something to do when all else fails. If you want life to be less of a struggle, pray first! The minute you experience fear in any form, a problem, a feeling of being disconnected from love, stop then and there, and pray. Turn your mind and any problems within it over to God.

Although in the beginning it is easier to pray when in a quiet place, you do not need to be anywhere special to turn your mind to God and ask for release. Many times I have been out running or cooking soup at the stove and noticed fear creeping in – an unkind thought about someone, a personal insecurity or a fear about the future. It takes just an instant to release it over to God in exchange for something more peaceful.

Pray to return to love

It is impossible not to receive a response if you pray to be realigned with the Boundless Love of your heritage. When prayer appears to go unanswered it is because you have prayed for something that you believe will bring you peace, such as asking for your lover to return to you, for more money or for someone sick not to die. If you look back on your life, you will no doubt discover that the best blessings are the ones that crept up on you without prior planning. Pray not for specific outcomes you believe would bring you the peace and happiness you seek, simply pray directly for peace and happiness. Trust that God knows best what that will look like for you.

Prayer gives you back to your highest Self. There are countless different methods of praying. The form of the prayer is not really so important, but the sincerity in your heart is. Having said that, this is the prayer structure that I find most helpful. Use it as a jumping off point until you learn just to talk to God and open to grace in your own way.

1 Gratitude

Begin your prayer by thanking the Divine for your blessings. Assume that absolutely everything you feel now, even if it is painful, is offering you a gift somehow. Be thankful for it.

2 State your intention

Speak to the Divine of your true goal – the state of being you wish to know. Do not be apologetic. Remember that God wants all good things for you.

3 Honesty

Tell God honestly what you are feeling, what you are thinking, and take responsibility for being the creator of your experience. The more honest and emotionally associated you are in your prayers, the deeper they will go.

4 Handing over

Give to God your problem, fear, mistaken belief or pattern that is in the way of your intention. Surrender it as though handing over a ball of knotted wool to be untied.

5 Releasing attachments to the problem

Give over any hidden motivations for staying stuck in the problem, fear, mistaken belief or pattern: what you may get from it. For example, getting to be right, superior, having the moral high ground or wreaking revenge over someone who hurt you.

6 Commit to trusting the higher plan

Give to God your commitment to true peace, love and happiness, not to conditions you believe would bring these things to you. Entrust God to lead you to your highest good.

7 Gratitude and blessings

Offer thanks for the immense love and help that is always given, and ask that all beings everywhere be receptive to Boundless Love and peace along with you.

Here is an example of such a prayer I wrote when stuck in a limiting relationship pattern:

Dear God,
Thank You for the gift that [name] is in my life.
I want to be free and happy, to love and be loved.
However in this moment I feel hurt, resentful and angry.
I know I am projecting past pain onto the present situation.
I give you my relationship with [name].
I give You the past hurts that are driving my defences now.
I give You my desire to be right.
I give You my need to blame.
I give You my fear of joining with [name]
I give You my fear of love.
Release me from everything that keeps me
Bound to limitation, suffering, blame and fear.
I do not know what to say or do to bring us back
To Love, but I trust You do and will lead me.
Help me see only the truth in [name] and the truth in myself
May all be released back into love along with me.
Thank You.
Amen.

No one can say any prayer with sincerity and not narrow the illusory gap between Self and God. It does not matter how often you become unstuck. At any moment prayer offers you a rope back to shore. Do not be proud. Do not struggle – pray.

'Oh God of second chances and new beginnings,
here I am again. Help.'

Nancy Spiegelberg

22

Acceptance: embracing your Self

'Pain exists only in resistance
Joy exists only in acceptance
Painful situations which you heartily accept become joyful
Joyful situations which you do not accept become painful
There is no such thing as a bad experience
Bad experiences are simply the creations of your
resistance to what is.'

Rumi

Self-acceptance is an essential cornerstone of a truly joyful life. There are two levels to self-acceptance: acceptance of the truth of your being as a glorious and limitless extension of Boundless Love and acceptance of yourself in the face of your egocentricity, seeming limitations and humanness. Both these levels of acceptance feed one another and through them you evolve spiritually and emotionally.

I meet many people on the spiritual path who are afraid of their own ego. The face they show the world is all 'love and light', yet their behaviour is often passive-aggressive. They often find themselves feeling stuck as victims or in roles of sacrifice. Trying to accept only your light while running from your darkness empowers the darkness with reality it does not have. Accepting your humanness and fears without reaching for a higher truth fails to transport you beyond them.

The combination of self-acceptance – embracing the highest spiritual truth of your being – and self-acceptance – extending non-judgement, forgiveness and compassion in the face of fears and ego patterns – will bring new depths of freedom, wholeness and ease into every area of your life. Most importantly, self-acceptance helps you to feel innocent again.

Your essence is already whole

Keith came for a course of spiritual counselling sessions knowing he was at a pivotal juncture in his life. A veteran of self-improvement, he had undertaken years of personal growth work, yet was re-visiting old feelings of self-hatred and despair. Recently separated from a long-term partner, he told me with great determination that he was ready to 'get rid of a load of shit'. He spoke of his own ego as though it was a gangrenous arm he needed to amputate. He had no love towards his own frailty: only thoughts of violence.

I gently reminded Keith that as the complete and already whole child of God he could dig all he liked but would find only diamonds not shit. We talked for a while about how 'working on himself' suggested there is something wrong with him in the first instance. I suggested he begin by grounding himself in the awareness that his essence is already perfect and seek instead to re-discover that.

On an emotional level, I could relate exactly to what Keith felt. He was fed up and frustrated with the inner voice of sabotage and self-attack that caused him to play small, feel insecure, withhold acting upon the truth in his heart, and behave in ways that caused pain. This fearful inner voice drove him to crack the whip and work harder, prove himself more, sacrifice himself further. He was sick of it and didn't know what to do.

Listening to Keith I recognised that classic ego trap of slightly twisting the spirit's desire to 'grow' as a good excuse to beat oneself up. This only makes your sense of guilt, fear and worthlessness feel more real, keeping the ego's fearful vision of Self strong. His desire to 'get rid of the shit' felt like he was preparing to wage war on himself, not open into a greater experience of love and truth. Keith had set a firm course for the kamikaze method of enlightenment.

I suggested to Keith that whatever we push underground

creates earthquakes later, and challenged him on his self-attacking stance. I told him, 'If I was your ego listening to you saying you want to carve me out, I would be digging my heels in and planning a few covert operations on how I could re-assert my dominance in your life.' Whatever you resist persists, and whatever you try to eliminate causes you to feel more ashamed. It affirms that there is an ugly dragon within that needs to be cut out or controlled if you are to be acceptable. It gives weight to the insane idea that there is something bad and therefore unlovable about you. It causes you to hide your light and to avoid anyone getting too close.

It causes you to stay closed and defensive, believing that if anyone truly saw you they would be repulsed and reject you, confirming your deepest fears of being fundamentally unacceptable. Upon sharing this, Keith asked me, 'How did you know that?' I replied, 'What makes you think you are the only one?' I knew intimately from personal and professional experience that the self-hatred Keith was facing was a deeply personal yet collective wound. One that no amount of self-punishment, self-discipline, or attempts to root out could heal, only loving acceptance would. Keith wanted to eradicate his ego, but you cannot hate your ego into non-existence. I reminded him that the means must be the same as the end.

Keith was afraid that if he ceased being so tough on himself his old patterns and fears would hijack his life. He tried to exert greater control over himself, only that left him feeling exhausted. While not indulging your ego and keeping alignment with your Boundless Self is very helpful, self-punishment is not.

Stop attacking yourself

Spiritually we are totally perfect right now, yet mentally and emotionally we are all works in progress. Everyone has rough edges. I have moments of selfishness, fear and insecurity. I sometimes step on people's toes when I am ignorant or not mindful. We all do. The problem is not in the existence of our limitations and ego attachments but our guilt and judgement around our humanness. Our ego tells us that we should be perfect, and then attacks us for falling short. This keeps us locked into old patterns.

Acceptance is vastly different from indulgence or complacency. Different from giving in, true acceptance is giving up. The irony is that whenever you greet a perceived foe with total non-resistance, opposing forces melt away. Without an enemy there is simply no fight. Whatever you accept integrates into a gift. What once seemed menacing transforms into a positive force that no longer controls but contributes positively to your life.

Embrace your dark stories

What is the dark story about yourself that you keep hidden? The story that says, 'If they knew this about me they would run a mile.' This is what keeps fear unnecessarily running your life. It is like believing there is a monster under your bed who will bite you on the backside the moment you let your guard down. Do not try to carve out or defend against this image. Instead try embracing it in the spirit of non-resistance and it will transmute.

Just as parents counsel their frightened children to turn on the lights and look under the bed to see that it is just an imaginary figure frightening them, so the way forward is not to run from your shadow figures and fears, but to find a way to embrace them. Then you will clap your hands with joy in the knowledge that there is no monster within and nothing to be afraid of because there is nothing wrong with you. The only way to realise that what you feared was an illusion is to look.

The primary reason that we run and hide from our fears is that we believe them to be real. The trouble is, the more we do this, the more real they become in our mind. The way to interrupt this vicious circle is to metaphorically hold the hand of God, and a friend or guide if need be. Drawing on limitless loving resources within or without provides the safety for you to be courageous, feel your feelings and turn around to face your fears. I promise that as you do so they will transform. Take courage from the beautiful passage in *A Course in Miracles*, which reminds us, 'If you knew who walked beside you, fear would be impossible.'

Embrace yourself now: a meditation

Sit comfortably in your sacred space.

✐ Light a candle and invite the form of the Divine to which you most relate, to hold you strongly. Ask also for your angels and helpers, if you believe in such things, to be with you. Ask also for the presence of anyone who has ever loved you to surround you. Ask for my love and friendship to be with you. It will be. Breathe in all the strength and support with each inhale, until you absolutely know you are not alone.

✐ If you need still more security, choose a positive context to lean into. For example, 'Every feeling contributes positively to me somehow', 'Every feeling brings me to deeper wisdom', or my favourite, 'At least my backside's not on fire and I'm not in complete agony as well as having this fear.'

✐ Imagine turning around in your mind so you are now facing your fears, dark stories or areas of shame, only you face them with mighty companions beside you.

✐ See your fears as frightened children acting scary to get your attention. With the help behind and beside you, walk towards them with your arms open, willing to give to these parts the love and acceptance they crave. Do not resist or try to change them, but embrace these parts exactly as they are.

✐ Walk into each dark figure, each fear. Notice as you do so, it ceases being scary and rises to bless you. Each fear or shadow you embrace leaves you feeling lighter, freer, more yourself. Keep doing this until all fear turns into light.

✐ Now ask to be led into a deeper experience of the truth of your being.

✐ Thank the love that has walked with you. Know that Boundless Love always walks with you, and that you can call upon it anytime you forget.

Holding the hand of love, you will enter a deep understanding, knowing that there is nothing that could ever make you unacceptable to God. You will discover that your innocence has not been lost to you. You will come full circle into your eternal Self, and that will gift you with greater freedom, peace and joy with which to gift the world. Your shadow need hide your light no more.

'To God, nothing about you could ever be unacceptable.'

Tom Carpenter

23

The choice to trust

'All is well
And all shall be well
And all manner of things
Shall be well.'

Julian of Norwich

Your faith is whatever you place your trust in. It is the seat of
your power. Whatever you trust in you align yourself to, and
magnetically draw to yourself. What are you trusting in?

You can never lack trust, but you can place your trust in an
unhelpful direction. You can choose to trust in your fears, in
your seeming inadequacies, in the future turning out just like the
past, in your own weakness, in other people's worst, in the
negativity of the world. Alternatively, you can choose to trust
that you are blessed and held within Boundless Love, and given
every resource in which to thrive.

In every moment, you are choosing where you will place your
trust. Wherever you place your trust you also place your power
and your creative energy. Choosing to trust in Boundless Love
instead of your own or others' weakness gives you the strength
and courage to handle anything. Choosing to trust that life
supports you, brings happiness, joy and the way forward to
your door. Placing your faith in limitless Divine resources within eliminates notions of frailty and impossibility, even in the
most difficult situations. Trust, appropriately placed, anchors
you to eternal grace while you walk in an ever-changing
landscape.

Whenever you rely on the 'strength' of your independent
separate self to get you through difficult situations you have

every reason to be afraid. Utilising limited resources, you have cut your self off from the supply of that which can help you. However, if you ask for help from God, from the Boundless within your self and all things, you connect with the limitless strength that can move mountains. Alone you are frail, bonded with the Infinite you are immeasurably strong.

Trust will resolve any problem

My friend Mary is a single mother of two living in rural Ireland. One of her children has severe learning difficulties. Divorce still holds shame and stigma in her conservative minded community, and Mary has little support. For three years she has been viciously dragged through the courts by her very angry ex-husband, and shunned by her family and community. For six months she woke up to abusive graffiti on her front walls and obscene rubbish dumped onto her front yard. It was deeply painful, disturbing and frightening. The police could do nothing.

Whenever it all got too much, Mary would phone me. A deeply spiritual person, she had prayed endlessly for the situation to change. It only seemed to worsen. We worked together on letting go the negative verdicts about herself that the actions of others would raise: Mary's feelings of shame, fear and worthlessness. The internal voice that would say, 'They are right. You're valueless, you're rubbish.' We prayed together to withdraw her faith in such thoughts and re-centre her in a deeper truth. We explored forgiving her ex, her family and herself. All this helped her to be more at peace, but the outer problem remained.

Over time something extraordinary began to take place within Mary. Despite outer circumstances, she grew stronger, calmer and more confident in her own goodness. One day Mary said to me, 'I don't know why this is continuing. I've done everything that I can on the inner and the outer levels, and I've given up trying to understand. I'm just trusting I can get through it, and that somehow my family and I will thrive. Although I cannot imagine how, I trust that some immense gift will come from this.' Mary shared with me a prayer she found over the Internet that was sustaining her in this vision. It went like this:

'Dear God,
help me to remember that there is nothing
that could happen to me today
that You and I, together,
cannot handle.'

Mary's situation eventually calmed down, but not before she had gained a deep trust in the process, in herself and in her own innocence. Choosing to trust in the Highest, even in the midst of such an awful situation, transformed her, and she became a beacon of hope and inspiration to many people in the process. Mary learned to put the power of her mind towards a positive outcome, without knowing how that would come about.

Trusting when you don't understand

There are many spiritual theories for why we go through what we do. Some say it is karma, the effects of our consciousness or the inevitability of being human. Who really knows why children die, marriages break down, people get sick or cherished dreams crumble? Personally, I take comfort in the idea that in the grand scheme of things I never know what anything is truly for. I trust, however, there is always grace in any experience, no matter how difficult I find it. Nothing is ever purposeless.

You may think the latest challenge is a curse that has come to wreck your life, but in a few years' time you may look back upon it as the soil that produced the greatest breakthrough. Why not assume now, that whatever appears to be going 'wrong' is an invitation to greater healing and awareness rather than a disaster? Ask inwardly for guidance and listen attentively for clues around you. Trust that things will work out perfectly, not necessarily to unfold as you expect. Trust that God's will for you is deep happiness, and that somehow what's occurring is part of the plan to deliver you unto it.

When you are hurt, afraid or disappointed, you will not feel much like trusting that life loves and support you. Yet, this is the time when you most need to withdraw your trust that, 'Life's a bitch and then you die', 'I'm unlovable', 'Men are bastards', 'Women want to control me', or any other fearful untruths, and align your trust in the Boundless. You will still have days that get you down. The occasional purgative moan session can be downright therapeutic, but indulging in it too long is poisonous.

For many people, trusting in fear, thinking themselves a powerless victim and moaning about how bad their lot is is a habit. Unfortunately, the thinking of the world supports it.

> *Ask yourself often:*
> * *Do I want to be host to boundless possibility or hostage to my fear?*
> *Never forget that these are your only two options.*

When you find yourself wallowing in fear, know you can stop and replace your trust in the Boundless whenever you want to. When you trust in whatever you most want to unfold: happiness, love, truth, peace, and not in specific outcomes, grace draws you back into the flow of life.

Boundless Love blesses you always

The most beautiful place on earth to me is a beach on the north shore of the Hawaiian island of Kauai called Hanalei Bay. Imagine a perfect crescent moon bay flanked by chiselled mountains, streaked with waterfalls flowing into the sea and with perfect golden sand and clear calm water. Whenever Robert and I visit out of season the beach is virtually deserted. We love to come early in the morning to meditate. One morning, after two hours of deep silence, I was opened to a most beautiful experience that vastly increased my capacity to trust. The physical world that I looked out upon became intensely alive with blessings. The boundary of separate forms fell away. It was as though everything I looked upon or came into contact with was whispering Divine love to me. Every molecule of air I inhaled, every grain of sand under my feet, every person I came into contact with, every creature in existence, indeed the entire universe was rising up to bless, feed and love me. It was a rapturous awakening to the reality of the absolute abundance of existence. I felt it mentally, emotionally and physically.

This feeling of being abundantly blessed was profoundly expansive and all-pervading. It took a while to integrate, but after that opening something deep within me relaxed. I grew less defended, happier and more trusting. Fearful states had much less sway.

Since then I have had many similar experiences of feeling the hand of grace feeding me. While I first opened to this experience in a place of great physical beauty, I have come to realise that the experience of the Boundless loving me can occur anywhere, even within the most mundane circumstances. Indeed, I have experienced it in the midst of absolute chaos. The more I allow myself to receive it, the more instinctively I can trust that no matter how it looks, all is well. As my trust grows, the more present I am able to be with others. The more I trust, the more I can allow inspiration to reach me when I don't know the way. Life has become much more fluid.

I invite you to trust that all of life rises to bless, heal and feed you in each moment. Consider the possibility that whoever is in front of you now is your gift from God. Consider the possibility that whatever situation you find yourself in is trying to bless you, even though it may be disguised. Consider the possibility that all really is well. Relax!

If you choose to trust in the Boundless Love within yourself and within all people and things, you can extract grace from anything. Life will become wondrous, blocks will clear and you will grow wise and strong. If you choose not to, you will remain asleep in the notion that life is a joyless struggle. Life will seem hard. This need not be. All trust will cost you is your cynicism and any beliefs that you may not be worthy to receive a beautiful life. Give these blocks over in prayer. They offer nothing that you truly want.

Lean into Boundless Love: a meditation

Over the years, whenever I'm facing what looks like an insurmountable challenge, our dear friend and mentor Tom Carpenter has counselled me to 'lean into love'. I find it such a helpful metaphor. Lean your mind into love like you would lean your body into the arms of your lover. Lean your mind into love in that way you lean your head against a soft cushion. Lean you mind into love in that way you lean your body into bed at night. Let Boundless Love become your soft place to fall. You can use this as a base for meditation when facing a challenge . . . .

 Sit comfortably in your sacred space, and close your eyes.

 Feel the support of the chair holding your body, and relax into it more and more . . . . Imagine that just as you naturally trust the chair to hold your body, trust God, the spirit of Boundless Love, to hold your heart, mind, soul and life.

 Relax and let life feed and restore you. Breathe in Divine strength with each breath. Just as your body moulds into the chair, your being moulds into receiving blessings, strength and grace.

Spirit of Boundless Love
Help me withdraw my trust in fear and place it instead in Love.
I lean my mind into Love, I lean my heart into Love, I lean my body into Love,
I lean my past into Love, I lean my future into Love
I lean my relationships into Love, I lean my work into Love
I lean everything I have into Love,
Help me trust in the Boundless Love within me
Help me trust in the Boundless Love within everyone,
Help me remember that
Nothing is impossible.
Thank You.

24

Surrender

When you are weary, let go, and I will catch you
When you are frustrated, step back, and I will hold you.
When you hurt, fall inwards, and I will heal you.
When you feel alone, listen, and I will speak to you.
When you cannot see the way, trust, and I will lead you.
When you let go, grace draws you back to the Real
There is nowhere for you to dwell but in my embrace.
Here you are happy. Here you are home.
Surrender, cease resisting, and
Fall into the arms of Love.

Peter McGhie was half way through the Interfaith Seminary training when was re-diagnosed with the lung cancer that had first surfaced 10 years ago. Initially, he returned to the lifestyle modifications, alternative therapies, drugs and fighting attitude that had worked to bring him into remission in the past. This time, however, life seemed to have a different agenda. Experiencing rapid physical decline, Peter began to face the fact that he was dying.

Feeling his way through denial, anger and fear, something within Peter gave way into deep acceptance, trust and surrender. Towards the end of his life he reached a rare, radiant state of being. He became the walking image of a free man: completely himself, present, deeply satisfied, open-hearted, playful and in love with life. A week before his death I felt inspired to post him a card with the words of the Sufi poet Hafiz:

'This is the time
For you to deeply compute the impossibility
That there is anything
But grace.'

These words sustained Peter in his last days. They gave him the courage to let go into the ultimate mystery gracefully. Having moved beyond his fears of what lay behind the veil of physical life, Peter had come to trust that the unknown was indescribably wonderful. Keeping his focus on love, something deep within him relaxed, and he entered a state of Boundless being. Fear departed.

Peter died a beautiful death on Easter Monday in the arms of his wife Nina and daughters Tanja and Natasha. Over his heart was the card I had sent containing Hafiz's sacred words. On his face was a smile. In Peter's dying, he inspired those who knew him, showing them how to live in a state of boundless being through surrender.

There are times in everyone's life when past strategies for dealing with difficulties no longer seem to work. In these times it is easy to despair and think there is no way forward, or cling to outdated defences. These are the times when you are asked to step beyond what you know, trusting that the hand of life will carry you to the next level. Arriving at the end of yourself and what you know is far from a disaster, it's where you meet freedom. It is where you meet a deeper truth, a new and better way of being. It is also where you meet God. Divine hands await at the edge of your cliffs.

Unfortunately, surrender often raises military connotations of defeat and loss. Yet it is the most positive and powerful step you can take to bring you into Boundless Love. Every aspect of living asks for some kind of surrender. Growth demands you release the old to make way for the new. If you cling to control and cleave to the known you will never grow into your truest self or your highest happiness.

Surrender to love

The word surrender comes from 'to render', which is to give. Far from 'giving in' out of weakness, fear or despondency, true surrender is a stance of strength where you 'give yourself over' into a higher state. Surrender yourself not to fears, but to God's Boundless Love. Surrender is not an act of passivity, resignation or defeat, but a dynamic act of courage that allows the next level of love, wisdom and truth to emerge. Not knowing the details of the way forward becomes irrelevant. God knows the way.

Surrender is the means for how you up-grade your life. To surrender is to give up something that isn't working any more for something wonderful, or to let go of something good for something even better. When you surrender yourself to God, you surrender to the creative force that moves the world. Just as a river does not need to be pushed to flow down to the sea, an embryo does not have to be forced to grow into a baby or a seed does not have to be manipulated to grow into a flower, no more do you need to force the events in your life.

Hard to trust though this is in the control obsessed western world, when you entrust your life to a higher plan and let go of trying to direct the details, things fall naturally into an order that works. Spiritually, you are built for greatness, love and happiness. Surrender helps you get out of your own way.

Surrender demands that you give up your attachment to the form you believe your happiness should take. If you embrace the principles and practices of Boundless Love I have described so far, I know that your life will become richer, sweeter, happier and more loving. Many unexpected blessings will come your way, but I have no idea what outer shape that will take for you. Often, the best parts of life are the things you could not have planned.

Start loving what is

No mistake you or anyone else makes can change what truly is – that you are loved, that you are love, and in the arms of love itself you are still whole. Nothing can ever alter the truth of your being. Accepting this makes surrender safe and easier. Grace loves to play catch with your soul. Knowing that there is nothing you could ever do to make yourself Divinely unacceptable takes you out of the fight with yourself. Let's face it: most, if not all, of your suffering comes about because you are fighting with someone within or without.

Surrender helps you to accept the invitation to miracles at your door. No matter how it is packaged, every event and encounter is a sacred conspiracy to bring you into something better. Life is trying to help you to be happy and free. Surrender is what knocks when you're done with trying so hard. Surrender liberates you from pain, and it helps you melt into who you really are.

Surrendering your strategies for something greater, you discover a grace you cannot know otherwise. The more courageously you let go, the more sublimely beautiful life becomes. Ordinary moments become more magical, and every nuance of the human heart more beautiful.

Surrender allows you to be

As you let go of control, tension dissolves. You come to smile at the Divine chess game that forms the temporary outer movements of your life – the people who come and go, the success that waxes and wanes, the dreams that rise and fall. Surrender takes you to the place beyond duality into the eternal now. In the present you discover that everything you truly want is on the table.

In return for the inner space you create through surrender, something Divine and powerful is unleashed. Something deep within relaxes. You realise that it is not necessary to try so hard, that you are okay. Your Boundless Self breathes. Truth rises forward to illuminate your vision. You can just be. This translates into an increased capacity to fulfil your unique function here, becoming a clearer conduit for loving assistance to others.

Surrender helps you open to synchronicity and surprise. The more you let go of control, the easier life becomes. What author Alan Cohen describes as the Cosmic Coincidence Control Centre can get to work, delivering you to your heart's truest yearnings and your deepest joy. Surrender your pride, surrender your control, surrender your fear, surrender your anger, surrender any fights you may be engaged in, within or without, surrender your attachments to specific outcomes. Surrender and fall into the arms of love.

A meditation on surrender

Sit comfortably in your sacred space and turn your focus within.

⟶ As you breathe, imagine that you are breathing in the love and support of heaven and everyone who has ever loved you. As you breathe out, let yourself relax ever more deeply. Breathe and feel your body become heavy, sinking into the chair beneath you. With every exhale, relax and let go some more . . . .

⟋⟋⟋ Feel a warm glow emanating from deep within your heart. Let yourself be effortlessly drawn deeper inside.

⟋⟋⟋ Sense a Divine being, an angel or face of God most meaningful to you, resting within that warm place within, its arms outstretched, calling you to just fall into love. This presence reminds you it is safe to let go.

⟋⟋⟋ Let yourself fall back into the arms of this presence. Let yourself be held completely and nurtured at the deepest possible level . . . .

⟋⟋⟋ Whatever you have been clinging to – an old hurt, an old fear, an old belief, an old habit, a stuck situation – ask this presence to, 'Show me a better way forward. Deliver me to a higher truth.' Rest in the arms of Boundless Love.

⟋⟋⟋ There is nothing you need do now. No more effort. No more struggle. No more trying. No more proving. No more fear. Just let yourself be delivered to your truest next step. Let love deliver you unto Boundless Love.

Beloved,
Love has drawn me close to my heart
Let me live from here now
I give my life to You and place my faith in love
I surrender my mind to You
I surrender my heart to You
I surrender my home to You
I surrender my work to You
I surrender my relationships to You
I surrender my body to You
Use me as You will
I trust You embrace me in deep peace
That I am innocent, whole and safe
That Your will for me is deep joy
So be You in charge now and forevermore.
Amen.

Part VII

SPIRITUAL RESISTANCE

25

Integrating gracefully

'It was but yesterday I thought myself
a fragment quivering without rhythm in the sphere of life.
Now I know that I AM the sphere,
And all life in rhythmic fragments moves within me.'

Kahlil Gibran

Whenever you shift from entertaining a spiritual principle to embracing it, new levels of love, wisdom and grace can integrate through you.

Emma is someone I immediately recognised as a treasure. A courageous, honest and humble psychotherapist in her fifties, Emma came for spiritual counselling sessions, wanting to go beyond understanding her own pathology to embracing her Divinity. Diligent in her daily spiritual practice, Emma nurtured and watered every seed of guidance I planted.

One day Emma said to me, 'I've spent years exploring my hell, and everyone else's too.' Emma defined hell as the times she had felt in a dark pit, alone, afraid, unloved, guilty, despairing, hopeless. 'Now I want to explore heaven,' she said. Excited by her boldness, I gave Emma a large sheet of paper. I asked to her to write down in specific detail her hell at the bottom of the page, and her intuitive description of heaven at the top of the page. 'Where between these two states would you place yourself now?' I asked. To her own surprise, Emma placed herself just underneath heaven. Together, we then entered a meditation on surrendering any resistance or fear of this experience, opening more consciously to heaven here and now.

Emma emerged from the meditation visibly moved. Tears of gratitude streamed down her face as she said in all genuineness,

'I've experienced my heaven.' Listening to her experience, I knew she had received a genuine opening not a fantasy. She described all form dropping away into scintillating light, feeling completely free, unified with everything, devoid of inner commentary, judgement and fear, resting within the bliss of Boundless Love. I recognised it well. It matched all accounts of life beyond separation I have received and heard of.

Without wanting to take away from the beautiful moment, I knew that this experience would require mindful handling. Being graced with a more expanded vision is one thing; integrating it is another. Experience has shown me that shortly after a big leap, spiritual opening or breakthrough, fear can kick in with a vengeance. I call it *Part two: the ego strikes back!* This is nothing to be afraid of if you know how to approach it. Your separate self does not handle change well. Without awareness of the integration process, it is easy to fall backwards.

Whenever you take a courageous leap, as Emma had, initially you feel very expansive. Be it a mystical opening, a freeing up of an old pattern or a new love affair, the process is the same. When a new world opens, you feel certain you will never run into petty problems and neuroses again. Feeling so wonderful, commonly you try to cling to the expanded experience, only the moment you do so it is gone. Just when you begin to feel indomitable, fear sneaks in the back door. Thoughts of separation and judgement can creep in, and quickly you can feel as though you have 'fallen from grace'. Landing back into petty judgements and fears from such expanded heights feels like agony.

The fearful ego mind, struggling to find its place in new territory and afraid of redundancy, uses this as a great opportunity to remind you what a spiritual failure you are. All the negative inner scripts come out: 'Not good enough', 'Nothing', 'Bad', 'Wrong', and variations thereof. Landing waist deep in self-attack, you can fall into the trap of doubting or invalidating your wondrous initial experience. All of a sudden, you feel like you are back in hell. Ouch!

I explained this dynamic to Emma, and suggested that if she began to notice fear, judgement or doubt, to accept it as a natural part of the integration process. I coached her to enjoy and be grateful for the taste of heaven she had experienced, but not to try to cling to it. Instead, to just witness whatever unfolded without judging it as right or wrong. Above all else, I urged her to keep a sense of humour about wherever she appeared to land while continuing to open to the truth. No matter what, I reminded her, 'Know that you are okay and that nothing can ever destroy your wholeness or a genuine experience of grace.'

When I saw Emma a fortnight later she was positively glowing, 'Everything you described happened, and I was able to witness my fear trying to invalidate my heaven experience. I was able to accept myself in it without getting pulled down by it. It so helped knowing that I could never truly fall from grace. I feel much more grounded in the knowledge that heaven is with me now.' Furthermore, she continued to experience expanded states of being in her morning meditations, and new levels of ease and joy infiltrated her daily life.

Grace is instant: integration takes time

Just as installing a new programme into your computer takes time to download, so your mind and body take time to ground and embody more refined states of being. Everyone has thresholds of how much grace, love, joy, bliss, blessings and ease their ego is comfortable with. To grow is not to be afraid of letting these thresholds be stretched. Whenever you experience an ego kickback reaction, relax in the knowledge that your ego faculties are just doing their best to accommodate a new state. This helps you to ride the process gracefully not get run over by it.

Until recent years, I had always dreaded my birthday. It felt like such a set up for disappointment and dashed expectations. Robert set himself a mission to heal me of this. On my thirtieth birthday he orchestrated an extravaganza celebration that lasted several days. On the eve of my birthday I was treated to a stunning concert from a favourite African band, and awoken on my birthday morning to a sumptuous breakfast in bed. The Divine even joined in on the conspiracy – my morning meditation was deeply blissful. The telephone rang constantly with loving messages. I received more cards than is decent. Family and friends were profusely expressive of their love and overly generous with gifts. I even received a generous cheque. I was wined, dined and thoroughly spoilt at every turn. Afternoon tea at the Ritz was followed by a thrilling West End show, which flowed into a fabulous late night meal with two close friends we bumped into outside the theatre. The day could not have been more abundantly joyous or loving. For well over 48 hours I felt so exuberantly happy I thought I would burst out of my skin.

Arriving back at the hotel at midnight I hit my joy threshold. I started to pick a stupid quarrel with Robert for no conscious reason. Thankfully, five minutes into it we became aware that I had found myself well beyond my current joy threshold and was experiencing an ego kickback reaction. It was as though some part of me was screaming, 'Red alert! Overload – must sabotage at all costs!' I laughed out loud, apologised to Robert, and we said a short prayer together asking for help in allowing us both to expand and receive it all more graciously. My joy threshold expanded to accommodate the present blessings. Ever since I have sat with the question, 'How much grace, love and joy can I handle?'

Two things will happen as you open to the experience of Boundless Love through spiritual principles and practices. First, things will get much better. You will fall into fewer traps. You will gain new clarity, peace, hope and vision. More of your best Self will emerge. Second, as clear water continually being poured into a mud-encrusted glass begins to loosen the mud and eventually flush it out, so over time, with consistent spiritual practice, old patterns and illusions will become loosened. After being flushed to the surface for your attention, they will gently release. Divine love is the most potent purifier there is. Sometimes, as a result of a greater opening, a 'healing crisis' is initiated. This simply means you are going through a process of release to move you beyond illusions and limitations into a truer state. Despite the difficult feelings that may arise, this is a very positive process.

Trust the process

Your unconscious mind has an in-built safety device. It will release to the surface what it knows you are ready to handle. That does not mean to say you will not be stretched, rather, it means that you will never be stretched too far. These are the times when you need to choose to trust the process and ask for plenty of help – from God, from friends you trust or from a spiritual counsellor or guide. Trust that if it's here, it's right. Trust that you are held in the heart of Boundless Love always, and thus are always safe.

In my experience, chunks of past pain and patterns have only come to the surface when I had the necessary maturity, solidarity or support mechanisms in place to handle them, though at the time I often doubted that. Take a positive attitude to whatever arises: celebrate the emergence of every old belief, old wound, old sense of feeling stuck or old fear. If you can recognise it, you can release it. First, know that it is only a mistake, never the truth. Mistakes can easily be corrected when brought to the light of truth. Second, trust that behind this lies a whole new level of freedom, authenticity, love, peace and joy. Handled mindfully, layers of old mud arising means life is about to get a whole lot better.

There is nothing more demoralising than an old pattern or pain returning that you thought was healed. It's the pain of 'not this again'. In these moments, the ego can try to convince you that you have not moved forward at all. Despair not when old patterns come knocking yet again. Remember that growth is cyclical not linear. Although you may be re-visiting an old pain or wound, you may well be revisiting it at a different level. Relax. Do not make a drama out of your drama. Complete release is inevitable.

Be patient with yourself. The forgiveness process I went through with my Dad took seven years in all. Moving from repressed little 'Miranda Mouse' to being able to communicate myself openly and confidently took place in several stages. Time, being an illusion, is irrelevant.

If you have to, gauge your progress not by the nature of what is arising in your life, but by the degree of equanimity, wisdom and trust you are able to hold within it. Whatever emerges in your life, make it your goal to keep centred, be at peace and keep your heart open with what is. You will soon discover that the heights you yearn for do not move away from you but are constant. Listen for the spiritual signposts guiding your way. Keep saying 'Yes' to what you really want, and smile at everything that may arise to prevent you accepting it. That way you will move through any resistance gracefully, growing back into your Boundless Self and into greater happiness.

In a nutshell

* **Be bold, and open to your Heaven now:** Remember that you are the only one who lays the limits.
  'Dear God, help me open fully to receive Boundless Love.'

* **If you experience an ego kickback, relax!:** Just witness the fears. Smile and accept yourself, wherever you have landed.
  'Dear God, help me to forgive myself and to accept what is.'

* **Know that nothing can invalidate your experience of Boundless Love:** Remember that you can never actually fall from grace.
  'Dear God, help me know that Love and Heaven are never lost to me.'

* **Commit to the highest truth, even if you no longer know what that is:** Do not resist your fear, but do not indulge it either.
  'Dear God, lead me from the unreal to the real.'

* **Ask for help in expanding to receive all the gifts life wants to give to you.**
  'Dear God, help me open up to receive every joy and every blessing you offer.'

* **Trust the process:** Choose to place your faith in the knowledge that all is well.
  'Dear God, help me know that whatever my feelings, You hold me and guide my way always.'

'Heaven is here, there is no other place
Heaven is now, there is no other time.'

A Course in Miracles

26

Spotting love blockers

*The only thing missing in any situation
is the love you are not giving, or
the block to love you are not giving up.*

Boundless Love is constant, the ultimate reality or your being, and the truth at the centre of all relationships, no matter how painful they may have become. Just as a clogged artery in the body blocks the flow of life giving blood to the heart, so learned ego habits can block the experience of love in your awareness and life. The problem is never an absence of love, but the traps you fall into that stop the flow of love.

To live in a state of Boundless Love, it helps to become aware of how you sabotage its experience. The only reason you may shy away from looking at mistakes is because you look at them through the lens of guilt, which obviously makes you feel bad. This need not be. Look with me in this chapter through the eyes of compassion at seven common love blockers. To recognise your mistakes is the first step to being free of them. Seeing clearly where you block the experience of love, you can ask God's help in letting it go for something better. Here are some universal love blockers, along with healing principles to help bring you back on course again.

Judgement

You cannot judge and experience love at the same time.

Your Boundless Self does not need to judge, it simply listens to inner wisdom for information and guidance with which to get through the day. Every time you judge anyone or anything you ingrain the sense of separation, and anchor guilt a little more. Most of your thoughts are judgements – thoughts of guilt, limitation, approval or disapproval about something or someone. So automatic has judgement become that you probably do not notice when you are doing it. Regardless of whether your assessment is true, every judgement you make interrupts your peace. It will tire you, cloud your awareness, and birth every other kind of love blocker.

I have not yet succeeded in getting through two hours without making some kind of judgement. Clearly I am not ready to let go of judgement addiction, despite my attempts. Instead, I aim to try not to justify my judgements and not to judge myself for making them. I know my judgement of others limits them and backfires negatively onto me. When I remember that I am not separate but one with everyone, I recognise that judging another is self-condemnation. Knowing this helps motivate me to let judgements go.

> *Ask yourself:*
> * *Who or what am I judging in this moment?*
> * *Is this judgement the truth or simply my perception?*
> * *What's the highest thought about myself, this person or situation?*

Instead of justifying your judgements, invite your boundless mind to reveal a higher truth about the person or situation concerned. Your judgements are simply opinions based on half-truths. It is not that you should not judge but that you cannot. To judge something accurately would require having all the facts at your disposal. Who ever has? Often when the bigger picture unfolds you see how wrong your judgements were. Loosening up your daily judgements is one of the most powerful contributions you make to a more loving life and a more loving world.

Comparison and competition

Comparison is an invitation to give more of yourself.

To compare yourself to others and compete with them for superiority is to place yourself in emotional prison.

From an early age you learn to measure your worth against another's. This cuts you off from your greatness, takes you away from your true being and dissociates you from your soul purpose. Born of unworthiness, competition causes you to dismiss the unique gifts you have come to give, and drives a wedge of separation through your relationships. Competition makes synergy, joining and win-win situations impossible. Far from bringing out your best, comparison and competition cuts you off at the knees.

For years I struggled with competition. I was heavily invested in being 'the best'. One day I saw that I was even subtly trying to be better over people I loved. This made me feel guilty and thus sabotaged my success. On closer inspection, I recognised this was my fearful self's way to keep me from showing up in the world authentically. I made an inner commitment to be more courageous, to choose to be my best and to actively support others in being their best, trusting that everyone can win. The motivation behind my actions became much purer, and ironically my life became infinitely more successful.

Ask yourself:
* *Who do I compare myself to/compete with and for what?*
* *If I simply showed up as myself, what do I fear might happen?*
* *What is the unique gift I have come to give the world/this person?*

No one can ever replace you. Just by being fully present to any situation as yourself, the Divine gifts placed in you by God become active and you bless the world.

Anger

Forgive your anger, just don't act it out.

To 'release your anger' it helps to understand what anger truly is. Anger is a defensive response to a hurt, upset, guilty feeling or heartbreak. Anger is the ego's attempt to 'make someone pay' for how they 'made you feel', hoping that they will see the error of their ways, apologise, be remorseful and cease hurting you. However, usually the opposite occurs. I have mentioned previously that anger is an attempt to make someone else feel guilty, and thus control them to change into how you would like them to be. Nobody wants to be made guilty and controlled into submission. Seen in this light, is it any wonder that anger consistently fails to deliver you into love? Do not make the mistake of thinking that anger gives you power. Anger enslaves you. Love is always your true power.

Ask yourself:
* Who am I still holding in anger (even if it is subtle)?
* If I let go of my anger, what do I fear I would lose?
* What is the real cause of my upset?
* Whose help could I ask to let it go?

That does not mean to say that you should not get angry. The fact is, everyone does. What helps is not to try to justify anger, repress it or dump it, but go underneath anger's face to heal the true cause of the upset. The true cause is never what it initially appears, but always an old wound or fear from the past being triggered by present situations. Spiritually, anger's invitation is to ask for help (from God, friends and guides) in healing the original hurt through forgiving yourself and others and communicating honestly. Then wisdom takes the place of a wound.

Blame, grievances and resentment

Holding a grievance is like drinking poison and hoping the other person will keel over and die.

Whenever you judge someone as guilty of causing you pain, justify your anger and cling to the past, seek help immediately! Nothing intercepts the experience of love faster than blame, grievances and resentment. Every time you blame anyone you declare yourself a victim and render yourself powerless.

Often, the grievance you hold over another is the very thing you cannot forgive in yourself. Blaming them allows you to hide from your own hidden feelings of guilt. No matter how seemingly justified, resentment is deeply unimpressive and only ever leads to sickness, sacrifice and heartbreak. The remedy is forgiveness, which is simply the willingness to let go of guilt and open to a truer perception. Forgiveness will connect you with more love than you believe possible.

Ask yourself:
* Who do I resent and for what?
* What fear about myself does this grievance hide?
* What do I want more: Boundless Love or this grievance?

Righteousness and superiority

Never make your belief system more important to you than loving.

If you need evidence for how destructive righteousness is you only have to look at centuries of religious wars, up to and including the events in New York and Washington USA on 11 September 2001. A close cousin of pride, holding a superior position of righteousness causes you to rationalise insane behaviour. No matter how enlightened you believe your opinion, faith or cause to be, if you take a superior stance, holding it to be the only true way, some kind of war or separation from love will be the result. Righteousness twists something that was initially very beautiful into something ugly.

To have passion in your convictions is wonderful, but to insist everyone share your views is to be a bully. Instead of trying to convert others, practice the essence of your belief with them. You can do this without saying a word. When Jesus said to his disciples, 'Go and preach the gospel', I do not believe he meant to beat everyone you meet on the head with Christianity, but to practice His teaching of love and forgiveness as whole-heartedly and as widely in each encounter as you can. Practising the fruits of your chosen teaching rather than imposing it onto others makes you a blessing.

Ask yourself:
* Do I want to be right or happy? (You cannot have both!)
* What am I trying to prove?
* How can I embody my highest belief in this moment?

Cynicism

It is never too late to embrace hope again.

Far from a sophisticated intellectual high road, cynicism is a negative approach to life that looks to find holes in hope to avoid taking risks and appearing vulnerable. Cynicism hides a heart that has been broken and turned numb to innocence and love. Cynicism is really just a mask for fear of being criticised and rejected. To hide this fear, a cynic dishes out criticism to others and attacks the courageous of heart out of jealousy.

Forgive those who once criticised you for your optimism and innocence, and you reclaim the courage to take emotional risks again. Dropping cynicism will make life so much more fun, and will allow you to feel loved for being you. I have met many people with a cynical 'tough nut' exterior, who eventually admit that they too yearn for Boundless Love. Cynics, be brave and come out of hiding.

Ask yourself:
* * Who first dashed my hopes?*
* * When did a part of me close the door on optimism?*
* * Whose help can I ask to help me follow my heart more?*

Busyness

'Busyness is a blindfold you wear when you are frightened to face something.' Robert Holden.

One of the most common methods for running from what scares you is keeping busy with endless errands, projects, meetings, phone calls, emotional upsets and dramas. It is a socially acceptable addiction that keeps you from being with yourself. Yet asking Boundless Love to sit with you as you face what feels scary usually discharges the fear. You are often left wondering what was so frightening in the first place.

Busyness also serves to distract you into love substitutes, tempting you to search for fulfilment in more success, more material possessions and more achievements. I have many professional and personal responsibilities, each of which I am passionately committed to. Unless I also commit to regular periods of reflection, which for me takes the form of twice daily meditation and at least half a day a week for being, it is too easy to get caught up in drama. Unless you make time to be a priority, looking within for clarity and answers, love will elude you. Choose to find the peace you seek.

Ask yourself:
* * What am I afraid I might find if I went within?*
* * What drives me to keep searching externally?*
* * What would make it safe to slow down?*

Returning into the Boundless

There are countless other love blockers, such as pride, inadequacy, addiction to dark stories, greed. All are just ways we enact the sense of separation from and fear of Boundless Love. Resisting God is the most unnatural, artificial act any of us are capable of. Our favourite love blockers represent the drama we unconsciously create to keep us away from the fulfilment of our happiness and heart's deepest longings.

You will know when you have fallen into a 'love blocker' because you will cease to feel that the Boundless accompanies you. You will feel limited, closed down and negative, and you will experience a sense of emotional distance from those you care about. As soon as you can:

* **Stop** and take a few deep breaths.
* **Ask** to be shown what you are thinking or doing that is blocking the flow of love.
* **Surrender** the mistake to God. There is no judgement upon you for wandering off course.
* **Return** to your centre – to your Boundless Self.
* **Listen** to your inner guidance for a truer way forward.

'Make it your daily discipline
to lay aside one little thing;
a tiny fear, a simple preoccupation,
a useless book, a piece of household clutter,
a habit of avoidance, a bit of shame or guilt,
a desire that distracts,
What will be left is Love Itself.'

William Martin

Fear of the light

Hold my hand.
Let us help one another not to fear the light.

For two years I worked with an exceptional client named Jenny. How she had survived years of nightmarish physical, emotional and spiritual torture at the hands of her parents and their friends I will never know. Jenny had lived through the kind of treatment no human being should ever be subjected to.

Highly intelligent, Jenny had spent years in therapy and had come a very long way. Able finally to cope with her dark past, the spiritual counselling we did together focused on helping Jenny not to be afraid to walk into the light. She taught me so much about my own attachments to suffering. We lent one another courage not to be afraid of the love, happiness, peace and freedom we most yearn, but to walk without fear into the Boundless.

A highly visual person, Jenny once described a powerful image she had received in meditation that graphically depicted her process. Jenny saw a ladder in a pit underneath the earth. At the bottom of the pit was the past with all its horrors. Above her in the light were the hands of friends, helpers and angels reaching down to help Jenny come completely out of the pit into the light of day. She felt immobilised half way up the ladder. In her mind it felt easier to fall back down the ladder into guilt, shame and her painful past. It took all her courage to keep climbing the ladder towards the light.

You are not your past

Logic assumes that we run from pain and cleave to joy. The truth is that we cleave to the devil we know, even though that may keep us in painful bondage. While consciously we yearn to step forward more into God, into deeper levels of light, freedom, love and happiness, our unconscious is often terrified of doing so, and heavily invested in staying put. The reason we are afraid to let go is because we have become identified with our experience, and thus attached to it, even when all it keeps us bonded to is pain. It is a dynamic that any seeker of the Boundless must become conscious of.

Robin had been on the spiritual path for many years. A graphic designer by day, he had spent years meditating and attending inspirational workshops. He knew all the principles, yet every so often would reach the same points of limitation. At these junctures old habits of struggle and fear would re-emerge to sabotage his progress. Gaining better support structures around him, over the period of a year Robin took many courageous leaps forward in his awareness and in his relationships. A whole new level of grace and ease opened up and Robin's life was beginning to flow as it never had before.

When the ego kickback reaction occurred, Robin's old patterns returned with a vengeance. I gently suggested that perhaps it was time to give up his *identity with hardship, his attachment to angst and inner conflict.* Initially very angry at such a suggestion, it took a few weeks for Robin to recognise that although his conscious mind wanted to continue moving forwards, deeper into the light of his true Self, another inner voice was screaming, '*Don't you dare try to take away my favourite place to hide.*' Robin then had to face the question, '*Who would I be without this?*' He realised that without his attachment to angst, struggle and conflict he would be free and happy. Robin eventually found the courage to allow that.

God holds your true identity

Often we come to identify with our experiences as who we are. The ego loves labels and stories like, 'I'm an alcoholic', 'I'm a survivor of abuse', 'I've had it hard.' Considering letting this go for something even truer raises all kinds of identity questions. Just when we think we know who we are, life challenges us to realise that our true reality cannot be bound up in any label. We can feel we are about to step into a vast reverie of nothingness.

The way to withdraw your allegiance to old illusions is to take refuge in something higher. Buddhists take refuge in three things: the Buddha (and all the enlightened ones that have gone before them), the Dharma (the teachings of truth) and the Sangha (community of friends who offer one another peer support). Whatever your chosen path or practice, learn from this excellent model.

To move out of the darkness of your illusions and into the light of greater truth, take refuge in your God, in the spirit of Boundless Love that is within you but beyond your illusions. Take refuge in truth teachings that remind you of your eternal nature. Take refuge also in friends and companions that walk with you into the light. Wherever you live, they will come out of hiding if you commit to not walking alone.

Often, just before you are about to move into a whole new level of awareness, temptations and old fears can come to try to scare you off. When the Buddha vowed to sit under the Bodhi tree until he realised full enlightenment, every possible demon came to tempt him away from his goal. He witnessed the temptations to lust, power and worldly gain and remained firm. Illumination was his reward. Similarly, Jesus spent 40 days and nights in the desert preparing himself to begin teaching. In his 'dark night of the soul' he was tempted to convert people by charisma and to claim Divine power and glory for his own personal gain. By choosing not to give in to these temptations but to anchor himself more firmly in the truth, Jesus entered his ministry with stunning power and purity.

Every time you hold firm to your highest goal and witness without getting drawn in by old attachments and temptations, the resistance transmutes from a negative to a positive force. The old dies off and you are raised to a whole new level of truth, power and purpose.

Dying to your illusions

In the East, particularly in Buddhism, death is not thought of as something terrifying and final that occurs just at the end of your physical life, but as a metaphor for letting go to allow something truer to be reborn. Hence the daily goal of practising monks is to 'die before you die'. Be willing to die to your self-concepts that a truer experience of Self can be reborn. Die to your fears that greater love can be born. Die to your past that the present can be reborn. Die to your hurts that your innocence may be reborn.

If you can embrace the metaphor of death as the letting-go of illusions that are no longer useful, making way for a re-birth, the moment of physical death need not hold any fear. You will know from experience that it is only ever the unreal that dies. The truth in you is eternal and indestructible. Anchoring your identity in God becomes the rope that pulls you out of any dark tunnel into the light.

The fear that light would destroy you is one of the most common traps of the ego. It comes from a deeply unconscious collective belief that we are sinful and thus deserving of Divine punishment. In my opinion, fearful religious theologies of a vengeful god simply reveal this belief that God is a frightening force that would destroy us if we let go our resistance. If fear of God's light did not exist in our minds, what could possibly be frightening about stepping forward into Boundless Love?

Collectively, we fear destruction of the Self we have created ourselves to be. We fear being swallowed up. At the deepest level, this is at the centre of every conflict, pain, trauma or fear of moving forward. Being stuck in some kind of limitation gives us an excuse to avoid the light of God, our true Self. That is why the past is less threatening than the future: the painful known more frightening that the potentially wonderful but unknown future. This leaves us with a split mind containing two fundamentally conflicting desires. It leaves us craving God's arms, yet running from them.

As deeply as I feel the ancient memory of Oneness, and have done increasingly throughout my life, in truth I am still afraid of it; although infinitely less so. I know fear of God's Boundless Love still exists because there are times when I feel incomplete, afraid and estranged, even though I know these feelings to be a lie. At a time when I was in the midst of this conflict – yearning to come closer to the home within, yet resistant and frightened to let myself do so – I wrote the following prayer. It continues to help walk me into the light of my true desire:

Beloved,
My heart's deepest longing is to dissolve into You
My mind's greatest fear is of being swallowed up by You
I seek Your loving arms yet I often insist
On walking the world alone.
Show me the courage to truly let go,
To cease hiding in my projections,
Distracting myself in games of fear and guilt.
Sing to my soul Your sublime song
Until I can hear nothing else.
Breathe Your breath through me
Until I cannot but breathe with You.
Take my conflicted desires
And purify me until only one remains;
To stand Defenceless within You without fear.
Amen

Every time I have faced my fear of the light, my fear of letting go of old attachments and false identities, I have risen into greater authenticity, truth and love. A new strength and power is reborn within me. It can for you too.

Is accepting the light blasphemous?

Who are we to accept abundant light, love and freedom? Who are we not to? Most spiritual paths speak endlessly about seeking on the path towards light. Sometimes this can become a trap. Like the carrot on the end of a stick, often we seek endlessly but do not actually find. Much harder to come by is talk of just 'opening to' the light. Remember that heaven is a state available to you here and now. You cannot possibly be unworthy to receive it. You do not have to prove yourself acceptable for it. Heaven was made for you. Accept the light that you may share it with others. Accepting what has been given you is not arrogant or proud, but truly humble. Accepting God's gifts to you is your acknowledgement of your source. Sharing what you receive with others is your gift back to God.

What do you cling to as an excuse not to walk into the light of your Boundless Self? Is it clinging to an old painful story? Are you still clinging to unworthiness to avoid rising to play your part in the Divine plan? Wherever you seem to be stuck is, at the deepest level, just hiding your fear of playing big. Do not be afraid. Whatever your special part is to play in the Divine plan, allowing yourself to rise into it will bring more fulfilment and more happiness than you can imagine.

 Moving on

⨏ Ask yourself:

> Is there an area of past pain that I still cling to as who I am?
>
> What frightens me about walking into the light of God and my true being?
>
> If I allowed myself to be that expansive, happy and peaceful, what do I fear I may lose?

⨏ When you have identified your fear of the light, remember that you always have the power of choice. You never need be a victim of your fear. Make the commitment: 'I will not use this to hold myself back.' You may need some time – hours, days, weeks, months, years – to commit yourself to this statement. That is okay. Take all the time you need.

⨏ Ask God, the spirit of Boundless Love itself, to infuse you with all the courage and safety you need to step into the light of your true desire.

⨏ Call upon the support of any teachers, friends, mentors and enlightened beings who have walked this part of the path before you. Call also upon the spirit of anyone who has ever loved you. Sense the immense warmth and strength and feel yourself held and deeply supported.

⨏ With all this support alongside you, see yourself planting one foot in front of the other as you walk into brilliant light. Walk into Boundless Love, Boundless Light, Boundless Freedom, Boundless Peace, Boundless You.

Know that your courage to walk out of your fears, illusions and past into the light is the greatest act of service you could give to humankind.

> 'Walk you in glory,
> with your head held high,
> and fear no evil.'
>
> *A Course in Miracles*

Part VIII

No
BOUNDARIES

28

Boundless relationships

'When the mirror of my consciousness became clear,
I saw my family and others I
love are the same as me.
The "you" and "I" thought
Does not occur.
The entire world is God.'

Lalla

I believe that relationships are the yoga for the 21st century. Yoga means 'to unite'. Every person we meet provides us with an opportunity to unite in Boundless Love. We should cherish one another as the gate to God itself. The old paradigm of cutting ourselves off from the world for years on end in order to awaken is outdated. Today, the spiritual challenge is to bring the clarity, the majesty and the sanctity of our inward seeking into our practical daily interactions with one another.

Consider the possibility that you do not end where your body stops; that you are a boundless being beyond constraints of the physical senses. In truth, you are unified with every mind and with the mind of God. As your spiritual antennae refine through spiritual practice, you can quite easily feel what others are feeling, sense when they will call, and know when something is wrong in their world. Your mind and soul is joined with theirs. Further still, those you consider to be 'other people' are really just aspects of your own being arriving at your door saying, 'Hello old friend, are you ready to embrace me? Forgive me? Accept me? Love me?'

If you were to see everyone as aspects of yourself, or God

in disguise asking these questions, and you were to answer compassionately, 'Yes, I will embrace you. Yes, I will forgive you. Yes, I will accept you. Yes, I will love you.' Could your experience possibly be anything other than Boundless Love?

There is one Self

If all of the mighty oceans and rivers of the world were drained, there would be no natural boundary between continents and countries. In the same way, our separate bodies hide the truth that our minds and spirits are unified. The vision of duality, where we seem to exist as completely separate independent beings, is an illusion. We experience it as real only because we identify ourselves as separate, limited personalities. Like individual facets of an enormous brilliant diamond, we are each unique aspects that make up one Self. Unity does not mean uniformity.

I have glimpsed our fundamental unity many times throughout my life, but was coached into a deeper understanding of it by my exceptional friend Tom Carpenter. One day we were walking together down Piccadilly in London during rush hour. Flanked by thousands, something suddenly began to open up in my awareness. Tom immediately felt what was happening and guided me through it. 'See no boundaries,' he said. 'Relax and see everyone as Self – as God. See beyond the body's eyes.' It was amazing how fearless yet safe I felt, and how wordlessly beautiful everyone became to me, even those whom I would normally feel slight aversion to. It completely altered the way I look at the physical world.

In that moment I truly registered that 'other people' are merely mirrors of various aspects of myself. In practical terms this means that 'others' will say what we think, especially the thoughts we do not voice. They will do what we are afraid of doing or having done to us. They will reflect back to us very honestly our inner state. There is nothing in your life but you and God. Anything that shows up is either a reflection of God and your Boundless Self or it is a reflection of a wound asking for healing.

Relationships reveal all

Consider the possibility that on a soul level, everyone in your life is your guru trying to usher you back home. They will either reflect back to you your true essence and beauty, or they are unconsciously illuminating what you need to heal. Listen attentively to the messages coming back to you from others. Accept as affirmation the love that is offered. Receive as helpful information the guilt, fear and doubt that's revealed: not that it is the truth about you, but somewhere in your mind you believe it true. To gain awareness of a mistake is to gain the power to let it go. Whatever is being reflected, the appropriate response is gratitude.

Ella was a 'fiery guru' to me at an important juncture in my life. When I first began to lead long-term groups, she attended a series of workshops I ran on forgiveness. A charismatic, articulate woman in her fifties, I originally enjoyed her quick humour, sharp mind and gutsy approach to life. I sensed, however, that underneath her personable exterior old wounds festered. As the months progressed, her defences became strongly activated, and she ended up projecting an enormous amount of anger and hatred onto me. It was intense, traumatic and well below the belt. In Ella's mind I became the symbol of everyone who had ever hurt her. Something within her went wild, and I received angry phone calls and accusative letters almost daily for a few months. Ella even wrote to colleagues, trying to destroy my professional reputation. Feeling responsible for helping open her 'Pandora's box', I accepted the slander because somewhere within my mind I felt guilty. It nearly broke me.

Knowing that such behaviour as this was actually a call for love, I did my best to stay in there and offer love and support in the face of her misdirected emotional violence, but it was very hard. Her accusations left me feeling I was the scum of the earth. My attempts to calm her down or make her go away were futile. Things only began to change when I approached her enraged accusations as a character within my own mind asking for self-forgiveness. This perspective gave me the capacity to extend the love I knew her rage was crying out for.

In my morning meditations I focused on embracing, forgiving and accepting the part of me Ella reflected: the thoughts in my own mind that I was evil, abusive, power-hungry, the worst of the worst. I had no idea those thoughts existed. I have come to realise they are there in us all. One day when she rang I no longer felt threatened, and heard myself saying genuinely without defence, 'Ella, thank you for your feedback. I appreciate it. I have heard it and I thank you. I wish you well.' That was the last time I heard from her. I had received Ella's soul gift to me and no longer needed to hear a reflected voice of abuse. Shortly afterwards I became a lot more comfortable with my own authority as a counsellor and leader. Ella had healed me of my fears of my own power. I trust that my acceptance went some way towards discharging her wounds.

Embrace relationship challenges

Every person in your life has been especially hand-picked from the Divine casting agency to help you somehow, even those who appear to be thorns in your side. It takes great maturity to trust this when someone appears to be wrecking your life. The key is always to look beyond the surface, inviting your Boundless Self to lead you beyond the appearance to the lesson at hand. This always moves you and the relationship forward into a truer and more loving place.

To my understanding, three categories of relationships seem to exist. The first category is people with whom there lies limitless potential for maximal mutual growth. No matter what you do, these people are always in your life. They tend to show up as family – parents, siblings, children, husbands or wives – or life-long friends. These are usually the people with whom you have both the strongest bonds and often the greatest challenges. I once heard someone refer to them as 'the unflushables'. No matter what you do, they simply cannot sink.

Approached from a unified spiritual perspective, you would never want them to eradicate these people from your life. They have more healing gifts to offer you than the highest avatar. These lifetime relationships reflect most closely the dynamic you have with God. Every pain you release in these relationships has a dramatic freeing effect on every area of your life, especially your spiritual awareness.

Love is never lost

In the second category are the relationships that are very intense for a certain period of your life, but seem to have a finite ending. They usually take the form of close friendships and love affairs. In these relationships the spiritual healing agenda is highly specific. Once the pre-set agenda is fulfilled and the lessons learned, you appear to separate.

I have found it immensely helpful to reconcile the apparent loss of a friendship or love affair in this light. When the 'other person' seems to exit my life I now see it as the fulfilment of a pre-ordained cycle, not a failure of the relationship. This supports me in letting people go, and brings me greater peace. That which was loving and truthful within your union lives on eternally.

The third category extends to all other living beings: the people whom you share the planet with but do not seem to be in relationship with, although in truth you are. You have no idea how profound an impact your smile, your kind word or gesture, even you peaceful presence has on others. I'm sure you have encountered people whose very presence lights up a room, and others whose state of fear or anger seems to drain it. Your inner state determines whether you light up a room when you walk into it or when you walk out of it. Every thought you have ripples out into the collective unconscious. Every pain you release in exchange for love blesses people you will never meet in ways you will probably never know. You are always in relationship.

Re-dedicate your relationships

Every person in your life will act either as your angel or your devil, depending on what you choose to be to them. Whatever the relationship dynamic, you are an active participant and have the power to bring it back into a more loving state. You do this not by trying to change another, but by changing your intention.

Consciously re-dedicate your relationships to serve the purpose of your Boundless Self, not your ego. Choose to actively reflect to other people the highest truth of their being. Be the angel that sees them as whole and inherently perfect. Refuse to be their devil by indulging in criticism and judgement of them, controlling or trying to change them. Whatever you give, they will return.

This does not mean you have to become 'best friends' with everyone, it just reminds you not to write anyone off. Choose to see the people in your lives as gift bearers instead of bomb deliverers. Question what your contribution is to them. Look closely as it can be quite subtle. You may not be actively acting nasty, but are you withholding your love if your needs and expectations are not filled? The principle of giving what you want to receive needs to be re-visited again and again.

Giving and receiving soul gifts

In relationships you are either exchanging your natural gifts, or unconsciously playing out your fears and wounds. Playing out one another's fears creates painful dramas. One of the simplest ways to interrupt them is to meditate upon these questions.

Intuitively, if I were to know what my soul gift to offer to [name] is, it would probably be . . . . Could I be willing to offer that quality or attribute from my heart to theirs now?

Intuitively, if I were to know what soul gift [name] has come to help me with, it would probably be . . . . On the inner level, could I be willing to receive that quality or attribute now?

On a soul level, every person in your life has an important gift or lesson to offer that will contribute positively to your awakening. You also have a gift for them that will help them into greater truth. Focusing on how you have come to help one another transforms any relationship out of separation and into love. The 'other person' does not have to do this exercise with you for a shift to occur, although it is great if they want to. Simply shifting your focus from exploring complaints to contributions will move you forward.

Beware of spiritual terrorism

One of the most common relationship stories I hear from clients and students is their struggle that partners, family members or loved ones do not share their spirituality. They make the mistake I also once made of finding something great and then thinking they need to convert the world to it.

Peddling our spiritual and philosophic wares at every opportunity is both a great way to become an insufferable bore and a direct route to loneliness. When what you believe or practise changes your life, others will notice. Then they'll ask to know more or your actions will speak so eloquently that you won't have to say a word. You do not need to share the same take on life to experience Boundless Love together.

As you commit more fully to your spirituality, you can often feel that you are growing apart from family and loved ones who may not understand your yearnings. Often they can feel threatened, feeling that they are losing you. Do not try to make others come with you. Accept your yearnings to 'speak the same language' spiritually with those you love, but give them the freedom to be who they are. Focus instead on practising increased acceptance and the heart of your spirituality with them. Celebrate differences rather than just tolerating them. Increase your appreciation of each person for the unique gifts they bring to your life.

Cease trying to be understood and, instead, apply your practice more deeply. In doing so you become more energetically attractive. When your presence radiates deep acceptance and appreciation, others will naturally feel less threatened. This may well open doors to sharing more of your spirituality. Remember that you can always ask for Divine help and guidance with any challenge. Know that a true spiritual life will always produce greater acceptance and bonding not separation. Let this passage from *A Course in Miracles* help keep you on course in your relationships:

> 'Whenever you meet anyone, remember it is a holy encounter.
> As you see him (her), you will see yourself.
> As you treat him (her), you will treat yourself.
> As you think of him (her), you will think of yourself.
> Never forget this, for in him/her, you will find your Self
> or lose your Self.'

29

Service

'When I am hungry give me someone that I can feed.
When I am thirsty, give me someone who needs a drink.
When I am cold, give me someone to keep warm.
When I grieve, give me someone to console.
When my cross grows too heavy and its weight I cannot bear.
When I need someone to hold me and it seems no one is there.
To lighten up my heavy load, give me someone who deserves
To be loved just as I do. Give me someone I can serve.'

Mother Teresa

This is the first half of Mother Teresa's version of the famous prayer of St Francis. I wept the first time I heard it. Not out of exhaustion at the thought of trying to live up to her stunning example, but because I recognised the profound truth she illuminates that true giving is receiving. It reminds me every time I feel in need, that the true fulfilment of my need lies in offering my love to someone.

When you accept that you are not separate but intimately joined to every person within the heart of God, you recognise that to raise another is to raise yourself. To ease another's suffering is to ease yours. The person before you is you. That is why every person who asks your help in any way is ushering you beyond your own fear into a deeper experience of Boundless Love.

True service dissolves separation. This is the fundamental principle of karma yoga: union with God through service and action. Mother Teresa, surely the greatest karma yogi of our time, saw every act as an act of worship, every face as the face of God. Embrace the spirit of service and you will both accelerate your awakening and bless the world. Every true call for help from anyone offers you a ticket home.

Step beyond your own limitations

Without exception, every time I have been in a dark personal tunnel for whatever reason, someone has knocked on my door asking for my help or called me in a distressed state on the telephone. Complete strangers have begun sharing intimate details of their struggle with me on a New York subway; people whose language I do not even speak have found ways of communicating their need.

Whatever form the call for love has taken, it has always spoken to my own situation. Until I understood what was really happening, my first reaction was often exasperation. Fear's inner voice would cry, 'Who am I to give to them in this moment? I have nothing to give. I'm a mess myself.' Yet somehow their true need would manage to pull the necessary grace out of me. Thankfully I had enough wisdom to trust the Divine hand guiding the process. Now, I am continually amazed at how intricately orchestrated the higher plan is. Whatever I need to face, heal or love, it appears in living, breathing, three-dimensional form in my daily life.

Whenever I give myself fully to another I go beyond my Ego Self and forget about my own problems. Joining with another in the present moment, the way forward emerges for them, and a shift takes place within me. Always, I am moved by the grace that has drawn us together and healed us together. These moments feel very sacred.

At first I did not understand how this occurred. Now I know that the fastest way to shift out of a stuck position is to serve some else. In heartfelt service you taste unity. That is why all healing is mutual.

To serve is to integrate

My husband Robert recently facilitated a great session at The Interfaith Seminary, during which he led the group into a reflective meditation around the themes of defencelessness, service and love. I paired up afterwards to de-brief with Kate, an inspirational poet in her early thirties. Kate revealed to me that she had zoned out of the meditation when it came to the theme of service. 'I've not paid much attention to service. I'm too busy working on my own healing. I will leave that until I'm further along the road.' I suggested to Kate that paying attention to calls for help from others and asking God how best to respond to them, was the means for her personal awakening.

As soon as Kate began to give her gifts in response to others' difficulties, a whole new world of creativity and clarity opened up for her. A new authority appeared in her poetry. Service carries you beyond conceptualisation to being. Whatever visions have graced you, they cannot be born into wisdom until you share them to feed another. Teaching what you discover by putting it into practical action, you become the teaching. Service helps you embody and master what you know, and stretches you into new territory while blessing others at the same time. Don't wait until you feel 'enlightened' to give of yourself. Giving will enlighten you.

Many people shy away from service believing they have nothing to give. They feel awkward, not knowing what to say or do. Thinking you know what to do or say in the face of heartbreak, death, betrayal or trauma often gets in the way. How could you possibly know in advance what words or actions are required in each individual situation? It is not your job to know the way. Just intend to be truly helpful, and do not assume you know what that means. God within you knows the exact form of help that is required in each situation, and will guide you. Your job is to align yourself as strongly as possible to the Boundless, be present and trust the guidance you are given. That is how you can be the presence of love that you truly are.

The morning I sat to write this chapter, David, a builder who had worked on our house a year ago, called around for no apparent reason. We are on friendly but not close terms. David is the father of two children, one who is physically and mentally handicapped. Severe birthing complications rendered his wife disabled. We sat down in the living room, and he told me that his wife had been diagnosed with cancer and told she had just three weeks to live. He broke down and sobbed. I knew there was nothing I could say that would erase the pain he was going through. I just held him and called upon the love of God as he cried. I did what came naturally. You don't need a Phd in psychology for that. David seemed to leave a little lighter, and I went upstairs to write, crystal clear on our need to love and care for one another.

In any situation, it is mostly your love and presence that are needed. Simply giving yourself is enough. Call upon the Boundless and intend to reflect to another the truth of their inherent wholeness, even though it may appear distant. Lend another your hope, your peace, your faith, your trust, until they can find it for themselves. Keep your heart open and your link to Heaven, and service will feel natural and effortless.

Service is not sacrifice

Where service is a natural extending of your heart and soul in the knowledge that others are you, sacrifice is a negative role you can slip into, thinking you are responsible for fixing other people and their problems. This thought is grounded in separation, and will quickly render you overwhelmed and exhausted. In addition, fixing disempowers the 'other' from listening to their inner wisdom. In sacrifice you forget that you are the instrument and God the source, and fall into the trap of trying to do the healing or helping yourself. Sacrifice is a form of counterfeit giving that hides feelings of guilt. At its darkest, sacrifice is a subtle way to gain superiority over others. It binds everyone.

The line between service and sacrifice is whisker thin. I cross it often. In the role of sacrifice, giving or helping becomes a chore. Unknowingly cutting yourself off from receiving any of the grace, you fall into giving for the wrong reasons.

Clarify your motivation for giving

I recently read an interview with the Dalai Lama where he described in detail his personal spiritual practice. Each morning he meditates for at least seven hours, two of these hours are spent clarifying his motivation for serving. I was humbled that a being of his awareness whose entire life is an act of service pays this much attention to motivation.

Whenever I slip into sacrifice, I notice that my motivation has subtly shifted from joyfully extending my love to others who I regard as one with me, to something altogether different. My ego sees 'service' as a means to:

* Look impressive to others.
* Earn spiritual 'brownie points'.
* Avoid upsetting someone.
* Give me a sense of being valuable when I don't feel enough.
* Distract me from facing my own issues.

Each of these dynamics warps service from an organic act of the heart to a means of keeping my illusions in place. Whenever you hear yourself saying you 'must' or 'should' serve, know you are coming from a place of fear and sacrifice, not loving service. Return to your centre within Boundless Love, and ground in the knowledge of your innocence and wholeness. From there you have two choices: either to follow what your inner guidance inspires you to do, or change your relationship to the request from 'having to' give, to whole-heartedly 'choosing to'. The purer your motivation becomes, the more authentic, natural and joyous service will feel.

Fulfilling your purpose on earth

The highest truth of your being is that you are the presence of Boundless Love. That you have come here to increase the level of love on this planet is without question. You have no option but to fulfil it. Never doubt that you have something valuable to offer.

The Divine has placed unique gifts and talents within you with which to play your part. I have yet to meet anyone who does not have something exceptional about them. Perhaps your gift is your courage, your capacity to love, your generosity, your humour, your imagination, your ability to communicate, your natural empathy, your intelligence, your vision, your musical or artistic ability, your capacity to nurture.

Ask yourself, and those closest to you:
* *'What are my natural strengths? My best qualities? My gifts?*

Though it may take you time to learn how best to offer your gifts, never doubt their existence. Your willingness to contribute of yourself lifts you into an interactive relationship with the Divine. You become not just a child of God but a co-creator with God, available to play your part in the healing of the world. In this you find profound meaning and happiness.

Some people feel called to feed the homeless or work to eradicate hunger, oppression or poverty. Beautiful though this is, service need not be something grand or overtly distinct from your everyday life, just a natural joining with another in the spirit of love. Give your gifts from where you are. Be open to everyday healing invitations and opportunities to give your love.

Every encounter is orchestrated with Divine precision. Grace will magnetically draw together those who have gifts to enrich, heal and help one another. You do not need to seek 'out there' for ways to serve, just pay attention and respond to those who come your way. Just give yourself. Give your love. That's enough.

Mother Teresa said, 'We cannot do great things, just small things with great love.' Make it your mission to raise the hearts and spirits of those you meet today through your warmth, your smile, your encouragement, your enthusiasm, your optimism, your kindness, your caring, your joy, your humour, your play-fulness.

Ask yourself:
* *Right now, what do I crave or need for myself?*
* *Who also needs this same quality or gift?*
* *Would I be willing to give it and thus raise us both?*

Inability to fulfil your appointed spiritual task is impossible. Just get fear and doubt out of the way, open your heart to whoever is before you, and ask God to act through you. Have no fear. God will take your willingness to serve and pour through you what-ever is needed. In the process, you will become the eyes, the hands, the heart, the feet, the touch, the mind of Boundless Love you were placed on this earth to be.

'When I need some time, let me sit with one for a while.
When my heart's heavy, give me someone to make smile.
When I'm humbled, give me someone that I can praise.
When I need to be looked after, give me someone that I can raise.
When I need some understanding, show me someone who needs mine.
When I think of myself only draw my thoughts to those who are kind.
When I'm so poor, give me someone who is in need.
When my eyes are blind to what is holy,
Let me see the Christ in each one I feed.'

Continuation of Mother Teresa's Servant prayer

30

Union

Let us hold hands with one another
And walk into a boundless existence
That transcends
Every idea of love.

As I look back on my life, I realise that what begun as a rapturous vision of Boundless Love in the midst of my deepest hell has increasingly become my daily reality. Gone is the broken and isolated young girl who forgot her Divine heritage and thus lost herself in the harshness of the world. In her place is a strong and open-hearted woman committed above all else to awakening completely into union with all that is.

My spirituality enables me to live a life of authenticity, inner freedom and inspiration. It has led me past dysfunctional patterns into an extraordinary marriage with my husband and soul mate, into deeply loving friendships and a transformed family life. It gives me the capacity to be who I came to be, and the courage to fulfil my soul's calling. It gives me the privilege of spending my days guiding others back into their wholeness and divinity, and directing an innovative training programme that empowers the new generation of healers and ministers. My spirituality has given me the capacity to live a life of Boundless Love.

Some say that I am lucky to 'have it all'; I know that luck has had little to do with it. Blessings come by choice not chance. My profound turnarounds are a result of my commitment to consistently apply the spiritual practices and principles of Boundless Love that I have shared with you. In the face of difficult tests and challenges I consciously focus on placing my faith in the power of grace within me rather than empower the fears of my ego. Though I still experience fears, doubts and difficulties, I know that I can dive within, metaphorically hold the hand of God, access direct guidance and thus act with wisdom when I need to.

I absolutely know that when you align yourself with the Boundless there is no lack, no limits, no barriers and no impossibilities. You and I are loved and supported beyond comprehension. The more I open myself to live from this awareness, the happier I become and the more available I am to bless and serve others.

Commit wholly to your spirituality

There is nothing you yearn for that is beyond reach when you commit to living your spiritual vision. Don't just think about it. Sit with God every day. Let your heart and mind open beyond the usual boundaries. Deepen your trust. Ask and listen to inner wisdom. Be bold and take the guidance you hear at its word. Bring your fears to the Boundless for healing. Call upon grace for everything. Join your mind with heaven and whoever happens to be beside you. Love and respond to calls to love. Embrace every seeming setback as a gateway into a new way of being.

The voices of doubt, fear and despair may still send their invitations: remember, it is not what is sent to you that determines your reality, but the RSVP you send in return. In difficult times, open even more to God and your Boundless Self and a deeper experience of love and freedom is bound to find you, for the heart of love itself guides you home.

Whenever I am in the presence of someone who is surrendering another fear, defence or mask, I sense a profound heavenly excitement, as though legions of angels are cheering, letting out a thunderous 'Yes.' This always calls to mind a recurrent vision that comes to me in deep meditation. This is the way I see it:

Within you is a state past all form and everything your mind has learnt. Like an ocean of scintillating light expanding into infinity, this is the light of Boundless Love. It is bliss without boundaries. It radiates warmth that reaches your very core and ushers in an ancient peace. From the heart of this light is a faint sound more exquisite than anything you have ever heard. It is the very song of existence, the essence of all that is. It sings of your essence and the true essence of everyone. Sung by the enlightened ones who have fully surrendered into this unified reality, they sing to awaken in you the memory of God and your Boundless Self.

Before fear and separation got the better of you, you lived in a state like this, and sung with the best of them. You will again. Your homecoming has already been fixed. It is only a matter of time before the illusion of fear and separation and all the painful experiences it spawns fall away altogether. Until this time, be courageous; risk living your heart's knowing. Open to receive the magnitude of the love that holds you. It reaches to touch you in all people and things.

Be in the world yet beyond it

Remember that the goal of spirituality is not to escape the world, but to live differently within it. Then will heaven and earth cease to exist as two separate states. The exact ingredients for your highest happiness and awakening lie within your present life circumstance. Hobnob with the angels it if helps, but do not allow yourself to go off on a trip. Remember that the Boundless Love of God and your true Self is a more unified experience within you, not another place. Your outer life can look very normal, while your inner state becomes lighter, happier and more alight with love.

Once you have consciously set your feet upon the path, there is no turning back. This love you now have for the Divine will never forsake you. The seeming veils between you and God will inevitably lift to reveal your Boundless Self that you may help guide this world deeper into the ways of love. For now, this is what is asked of you:

* **See God everywhere:** See God in the face reflected back at you in the mirror, in the face of your family and loved ones, in the face of those you work with, and even in the face of apparent villains.
* **Remember the truth of who you are:** by actively seeking out the true innocence and wholeness of everyone else.

* **Re-centre often**: It does not matter how often you fall off-course. The peace of your Boundless Self is just a prayer away.
* **Consciously commune daily with God**: Let your soul be fed so that inner wisdom may reach you. In the quietness your trust will grow.
* **Above all else – love**: Let nothing be more important to you than your choice to love the Divine, your Self and others.

The experience of Boundless Love awaits you. Even the most painful wounds can give way to deep connection, wisdom and laughter. You will know a graced life. Now is the time to walk hand in hand with the ones you love into the fulfilment of your deepest yearnings.

'Playfully, you hid from me.
All day I looked.
Then I discovered
I was you,
And the celebration
Of That began.'

Lalla

Further information

For further details about:

* Miranda Holden's *Soul Healing* series of guided meditation tapes
* Miranda Holden's private sessions
* The Interfaith Seminary
* Finding a spiritual counsellor or Interfaith Minister in your area

please contact:

The Interfaith Seminary office
Elms Court
Chapel Way
Oxford OX2 9LP
Tel: 01865 244835
Fax: 01865 248825
E-mail: newseminary@community.co.uk
Website: www.newseminary.org.uk

For information about:

* Miranda Holden's public workshops and talks
* Other talks, workshops and products from the Happiness Project team

contact:

The Happiness Project
Elms Court
Chapel Way
Oxford OX2 9LP
Tel: 01865 244414
Fax: 01865 24882
E-Mail: hello@happiness.co.uk
Website: www.happiness.co.uk

Recommended listening: audio tapes

Soul Healing Guided Meditation Series: Miranda Holden
Being Good Enough
Accepting Joy
Forgiveness: Transforming Difficult Relationships
Letting go of the Struggle
Choosing Peace

Audio series: *Robert Holden*
Ph.D in Joy
Happiness is a way of Travelling
Making a Success of your Life
Carpe Diem – Living Life Well
Inner Smile Meditation
Everyday Abundance
Success Intelligence

Recommended reading

Anon (1975) *A Course In Miracles*. Penguin Arkana.

Barks, Coleman (1997) *The Illuminated Rumi*. Bantam.

Barks, Coleman (1992) *Naked Song: Lalla*. Maypop Books.

Berke, Diane (1995) *The Gentle Smile*. Crossroad.

Carpenter, Tom (1992) *Dialogue on Awakening*. Carpenter Press.

Cohen, Alan (1996) *A Deep Breath of Life*. Hay House.

Cohen, Alan *The Dragon Doesn't Live Here Anymore*. Hay House.

Dass, Ram & Gorman, Paul (2000) *How Can I Help?* Alfred A. Knopf.

Easwaran, Eknath trans. (1987) *The Upanishads*. Nilgiri Press.

Gibran, Kahlil (1994) *The Beloved*. Penguin Arkana.

Harvey, Andrew (2000)*The Direct Path*. Rider.

Harvey, Andrew (1996)*The Essential Mystics*. HarperCollins.

Holden, Robert (1998) *Happiness Now*. Hodder & Stoughton.

Holden, Robert (2000) *Shift Happens*. Hodder & Stoughton.

Jeffers, Susan (1996) *End the Struggle and Dance with Life*. Hodder & Stoughton.

Jeffers, Susan (1991) *Feel the Fear and Do it Anyway*. Vermilion.

Kornfield, Jack (1993) *A Path with Heart*. Rider.

Ladinsky, Daniel (1999) *The Gift: Poems by Hafiz the great Sufi Master.* Penguin Arkana.

Ladinsky, Daniel (1996) *I Heard God Laughing: Renderings of Hafiz.* Dharma Printing Company.

Ladinsky, Daniel trans (1996) *The Subject tonight is Love. Hafiz.* Pumpkin House.

Perry, Robert (1993) *Guidance: Leading the Inspired Life.* The Circle of Atonement.

Ramakrishna Vivekananda (1942)*The Gospel of Sri Ramakrishna.* Ramakrishna Vivekananda Centre.

Rinpoche, Sogyal (1993)*The Tibetan Book of Living and Dying.* Rider.

Smith, Huston (1991)*The World's Religions.* HarperCollins.

Spezzano, Chuck (1999) *If it hurts, it isn't love.* Hodder & Stoughton.

Spezzano, Chuck (2000) *Wholeheartedness.* Hodder & Stoughton.

Spezzano, Lency (2000) *Make way for Love.* Psychology of Vision Press.

Titmuss, Christopher (2000) *Light on Enlightenment.* Rider.

Williamson, Marianne (1992) *A Return to Love.* Thorsons.

Williamson, Marianne (1994) *Illuminata.* Rider.

Wilson, Paul (2000) *Calm for Life.* Penguin.

Yogananda, Paramahansa (1987) *Autobiography of a Yogi.* Rider.

Yogananda, Paramahansa (1975) *Whispers from Eternity* Self-Realisation Fellowship.